Are YOU The Missing Piece?

Don't Leave a Hole in the World!

Journal with International
Best-Selling Authors to Change
Lives Across the Globe

Compiled by Viki Winterton

Are YOU The Missing Piece
Don't Leave a Hole in the World!

©2017 by Viki Winterton

Expert Insights Publishing
8640 University City Blvd., Suite A-3 #247
Charlotte, NC 28213

Compiled by: Viki Winterton

Cover Design: Terry Z

Edited by: Pam Murphy

15 14 13 12 11 1 2 3 4 5

A portion of the proceeds from this book is donated to the Santiago Foundation, a registered not-for-profit organization (US & Mexico), which supports education and trade training for young people and adults to expand their skills and opportunities. santiagofoundation.net

"There are no extra pieces in the universe.
Everyone is here because he or she has a place to fill,
and every piece must fit itself into the big jigsaw puzzle."

~ Deepak Chopra

Introduction
By Dr. Marilyn Joyce

It's your specific path ... not anyone else's path ... your unique and cosmic purpose for being here now.

We are each, individually, one specific piece of that cosmic jigsaw puzzle called Life ... and the Universe. And when we fit perfectly into our own unique, one spot only, space in this cosmic jigsaw puzzle, with grace and ease, and without apology, we are then one with our divine purpose, our mission, our reason for *being here now!*

Without your contribution to this cosmic jigsaw puzzle, it is incomplete, and will always be seeking its missing piece ... YOU!

Until you realize, embody and fulfill your missing piece in this puzzle, the global and universal mission of the whole is stunted, stopped in its tracks, and cannot be completed!

So, don't wait another minute! We need YOU ... the Universe needs YOU... NOW!

In 1985, when she was at the peak of her career and feeling like she had achieved the ultimate success, **Dr. Marilyn Joyce** was diagnosed with melanoma. She was shocked to discover how serious that illness was, and as if that wasn't enough, a week out of hospital, she was rushed back in again with stage four uterine cancer. She was only 35 years old! After she passed the initial shock of the diagnosis, she tried everything she could in search of a magic bullet. Yet four years later, she was in a wheelchair at 88 pounds, and according to doctors, with only a week-and-a-half to live.

Since recovering from those challenging cancer years, she has poured her heart and soul into learning everything she can about creating energy and vitality in only 5-minute segments throughout the day - often the only time a cancer patient, caregiver or healer has available at any given moment. Now after 27 years, Marilyn is one of the world's leading experts on *INSTANT E.N.E.R.G.Y.™: The 5 Keys to Unlimited Energy & Vitality!*

Dr. Marilyn Joyce aka *The Vitality Doctor™*, is a Best-Selling Author, an Award-Winning Speaker, Founder of Compassionate Cancer Concierge™, Kick Cancer In The Can® and Journey of 1000 Days and Catalyst for Global Peace. She is also the Co-Founder and Creative Director for Ecosse Publishing. JourneyOf1000Days.Love

— *DAY 1* —

*"'Missing: Lost, Absent, Misplaced, Mislaid, Gone, Omitted, Disappeared.' If any of these describe you, then it's time to take stock of what you can do to ensure that you are Present, Current, Contemporary, Existing or at least Nearby. Decide for yourself that **this is YOUR** time, **YOUR** moment and make sure that you seize **TODAY** to show the world how **you** being present and whole, not a piece, makes a real difference to the creation."*

Susie Briscoe, Founding Chair Acer Coaching Associates; International Business Executive Coach & Mentor; Master Leadership with Legacy Mentor; Author of 4 International #1 Bestseller books. AcerCoachingAssociates.com

My Inspired Thoughts

— _DAY 1_ —

My Inspired Thoughts

— DAY 2 —

"With advertising, you pay for it. With publicity, you pray for it. You need all four legs of the publicity chair — print, radio, television and internet.

When you do something just to make money, it is almost always the wrong decision. There's got to be something else driving you. It's got to be fun. You've got to be giving back. You've got to be helping people. If you do that, then the money will follow."

Rick Frishman, Best-Selling Author, Publisher and Speaker, Founder of Author 101 University, the Premier event for marketing and publishing success.   Author101University.com

My Inspired Thoughts

— _DAY 2_ —

My Inspired Thoughts

— *DAY 3* —

"Make money fall in love with you.

When you imagine your money as a real, flesh and blood person, worthy of your deepest admiration, you embark on an amazing, love-at-first-sight affair of the heart.

Pennies on the ground are like chocolates on your pillow."

Morgana Rae is a sought after teacher, speaker and pioneer in personal development and is widely regarded to be the world's leading Relationship with Money Coach.
MorganaRae.com

My Inspired Thoughts

— <u>DAY 3</u> —

My Inspired Thoughts

"I don't believe that you should do any-thing unless it can bring you joy and be a benefit to other people. I believe that the world is in such a state that each and every one of us needs to show compassion and generosity and be willing to give back, and be a shining light to other people. If I accomplish that, I will have accomplished everything."

Frances Morfin Koll, Songstress, Actor, Writer and Activist. Look for Fran's exclusive nightclub, Manhattan on the Rocks, opening soon in Manzanillo, Mexico.
fsongbird14@aol.com

My Inspired Thoughts

— <u>DAY 4</u> —

My Inspired Thoughts

— DAY 5 —

"I recommend travel because we are supposed to know each other. When I arrive in a new place with little money, no place to stay and don't speak the language, I discover I am never really lost. I find a place to sleep, something to eat, challenges show up and are met and then I return home. I come home with pictures and stories and secretly know I can go any-where and do anything!"

Devin Galaudet is the founder and Publisher of *In The Know Traveler* and five other online travel magazines. He has visited over 80 countries worldwide! InTheKnowTraveler.com

My Inspired Thoughts

— _DAY 5_ —

My Inspired Thoughts

"Life is a continuum of journeys. Each journey contributes to our character and helps make us the person we are. A destination is but a way point along our journey. Happiness requires that we recognize and embrace the journey. Without that, we risk savoring only a few fleeting moments at a destination rather than the hours we spent on the journey. Recognize the journey! Embrace it!"

Dr. Dane Russo spent 38 years working at NASA's Johnson Space Center in Houston. He now lives with his wife Jean in Manzanillo Mexico. bbcards46@hotmail.com

My Inspired Thoughts

— DAY 6 —

My Inspired Thoughts

"It is very difficult in contemporary society to stay away from TV, international gossip and the terrible news of so many wars and killings in our world that unfortunately lead into anxiety and depression having the feeling of not being able to do something. I invite you to dance with me and be able to understand what it means every step in your life."

Elizabeth Torres is an international dance council CID UNESCO scientific committee member, has received national and international recognition for this dance research work, and travels the world presenting ancient traditions.
tezcaxx1@yahoo.com

My Inspired Thoughts

— DAY 7 —

My Inspired Thoughts

— DAY 8 —

"The word foregone – yet manifold more, the actual, much-limiting concept – should be an unacceptable non-entity. Nothing is – nor should be thought of as – pre-destined or definite. For while successes' accolades, awards and honorifics are fine but fleeting, true accomplishment comes from within ourselves, knowing we have substantively surpassed all manner of expectations. Be these a standard striking-ly raised, a goal attainment level (heretofore unperceived) much enhanced or a heralded achievement exceeded. Our potential is limitless."

Tommy & Patty Clarkson. As a tutor, teacher, mentor, university professor and, even, combat zone correspondent, Tommy's consistent counsel regarding word usage has been to clearly "Paint a picture!" OlaBrisaGardens.com

My Inspired Thoughts

— DAY 8 —

My Inspired Thoughts

"I was warned, 'You're not going to make money selling books. You're going to make money by having a book and using it to close more deals.' That has been my experience – an experience far exceeding my goals and my vision!

When you do what you love, and you do it in the company of visionaries and household names, you become an instant expert in your field. You owe it to the world to get your story out in a book."

Viki Winterton, Publisher, #1 International Best-Selling Author, and Founder of Expert Insights Publishing. ExpertInsightsPublishing.com

My Inspired Thoughts

— _DAY 9_ —

My Inspired Thoughts

"Music feeds the soul and provides the melody that inspires in me love and respect for all living things. Meaning and growth is everywhere, as long as we are grateful for all our blessings and can revel in the music that lifts our spirit and brings joy. By continuing to learn, share and, yes, practice and develop new repertoire, I stay disciplined, curious, adventurous, and young."

Irving Colacci studied classical piano, dove into sex/drugs/ Rock & Roll, took a 25-year sojourn into corporate law and business then returned to his passion – playing jazz piano. IrvingColacci@gmail.com

My Inspired Thoughts

— _DAY 10_ —

My Inspired Thoughts

"Passion unites us with our creative authentic self. Finding meaning and purpose in our lives are innate desires essential for self-discovery. Creative inspiration is sparked by wonder, curiosity and spontaneity. Listen to your heart. It will guide you on the path that resonates with your soul to realize your life's purpose. Genuine expression of our unique gifts and talents fulfill our desires, eliminate the void, and serves humanity for the greater good."

Dr. Jean Farish, Award-Winning Transformational Author, Founder and CEO of Life Care Wellness/PEP For Angels, Inc. - "Enriching Lives and Serving Our Community."
jeanfarishjourney.com

My Inspired Thoughts

— DAY 11 —

My Inspired Thoughts

"If there is a will, there is a way for almost any accomplishment, but do not waste your time on incidental tasks that nearly anyone else can do faster or better. **Can't** *is not a four-letter word; pick your battles and let people help you with the tasks that you struggle with or that do not bring you joy. Put your self-reliance in your pocket and welcome the kindness that others want to share."*

Susanne Whited, Owner of <u>MyBusinessTweets.com</u>, helps business owners escape marketing madness to focus on practical solutions to grow their business through strategy consultations, educational programs and done-with-you services.

My Inspired Thoughts

— _DAY 12_ —

My Inspired Thoughts

— DAY 13 —

"Life's a wondrous puzzle.

Billions of pieces imprinted with a part of this collective, breath-taking artwork.

But: this pièce de résistance can only be completed when each tab interlocks delicately with another blank slot, a perfect fit, according to its design and purpose.

Each different, distinct, with a specific colour, shape and form.

Yet every one absolutely needed, assembled pieces sticking together, to fulfill the whole."

Ursula Nieuwoudt is an Int'l Best-Selling Co-Author and Author of *Practical Conversations About Fitting In*. She is working on her next book about diamonds. UrsulaNieuwoudt.com

My Inspired Thoughts

My Inspired Thoughts

"Imagine the world of oneness and diversity, where all are equal, but different; where everybody is free to be unique expressions of consciousness; where joyful presence is the new norm and where new ways of being are emerging effortlessly from playful curiosity. What would it take to make this true? What if this was possible NOW?

It all starts with you. You can be whatever you want to be. Choose anew in every moment!"

Metka Lebar, Founder of Foundation for Creative Thinking and Ecology of Mind, is a best-selling author, inspirational speaker, healer, workshop leader, consciousness facilitator, life and creativity coach. AccessOneness.com

My Inspired Thoughts

My Inspired Thoughts

"With Character All is Gained, Without It All is Lost. The end of education is character. School plays the greatest role in a student's character journey to earn this priceless credential from the education system. It helps corporations as the end beneficiary to build a credible workforce. Hence corporations must symbiotically rally in this character crusade with all stakeholders to produce students with positive attitudes and behaviors as the true wealth of a nation."

Asohan Satkunasingham is an Author, International Award-Winning Human Resource Practitioner, International Speaker, Human Resources Consultant and Builder of People Capabilities. abofcharacter.com

My Inspired Thoughts

— _DAY 15_ —

My Inspired Thoughts

— *DAY 16* —

"To dream is where plans are made. Hard work is where dreams become a reality. People come to me for hope, confidence, skills, and abilities. I love watching people succeed. I choose to work with leaders, people who are the movers and shakers of our world. Connecting them with solutions. As a creative and business coach, my fingerprint in the world is to assist others to achieve their dreams. Whether motivating or legendary, Dream Big!"

Rev. Dr. Tracy Elman, D.D, D.M., multi-award winning best-selling author, narrator and founder of Leap To New Heights, Empowerment for Life, Education & Coaching. LeapToNewHeights.com

My Inspired Thoughts

— *DAY 16* —

My Inspired Thoughts

'"Solutions to life's toughest challenges are but one dream away.'
'We always act to bring about a feeling within ourselves, yet we tend to miscon-strue that what we want is instead some-thing out there.'
'If you want life easier, remind yourself of the greatness you can grow into and later enjoy sharing with others, then dance ahead gracefully, embracing the gifts of growth life offers.'
'Receiving gracefully, we offer another the gift of giving.'"

Craig Sim Webb, Leadership speaker/trainer, and bio-medical inventor with empowering tools sold worldwide. Invited expert for major motion pictures, top celebrities, CEOs, and 1000+ international media.
DreamsBehindtheMusic.com

My Inspired Thoughts

— DAY 17 —

My Inspired Thoughts

"You cannot worry about the past, what has been. You can only focus on the future, what will be. If you dwell on what has been, you'll miss what can be. Always do your best. You never know who might be watching. It can lead to amazing opportunities and open doors you never imagined. Be persistent – keep doing! Always be willing to take a risk. Most of all, never let anyone kill **your** *dreams."*

David Medansky, Best-Selling Author, World Class Expert and trusted advisor on playing and winning at casino Craps (Yes, the dice game), and Attorney.   dmedansky.com

My Inspired Thoughts

— *DAY 18* —

My Inspired Thoughts

"Think you've outlived your success? That everyone wants the new and upcoming expert/thought leader? Not so. Not everyone in your whole tribe will stay with you till the end; they never do. But those you are meant to help, those for whom YOU are the missing puzzle piece — they take refuge in you, allowing you to fulfill your deepest purpose by giving them the perfect message at the perfect time to carry them forward."

A Divine healer, **Allura Adelson** helps 50+ Goddesses find ageless wisdom, healing, beauty, unparalleled growth and joy in the best half of life.   FindingYourBlissAfter50.com

My Inspired Thoughts

— *DAY 19* —

My Inspired Thoughts

— *DAY 20* —

"Prayer is fine for most short-term situations or health problems. Major crises and long-term difficulties require more than prayer and well wishes. Results happen quickly when people get involved by giving of their time, donations, transportation, and kind words of encouragement. The longer people have to wait for help, the more desperate their situation becomes. It also makes it more difficult to climb out of or to cope with. Please become that missing piece!"

Lorraine Price is a Book Coach, Author, Proofreader, Book Reviewer, and Speed Reader. Her interests lie in helping people, animals, eating healthy and becoming self-sufficient. Lprice9559@gmail.com

My Inspired Thoughts

— <u>*DAY 20*</u> —

My Inspired Thoughts

— DAY 21 —

"Shangri-Love is that place of unconditional love within your heart. You find it when you surrender to the present moment and allow life to be as it is while activating radical self-compassion. So get silent and be still often! Deeply listen within. Your heart will gently move to the forefront of your life navigation system and you'll begin to live the love story within you with peace and grace, regardless of outside circumstances."

Zemirah Jazwierska, Ed.S., RScP, is an empowerment coach, psychologist, licensed spiritual practitioner, meditation facilitator and author of *Shangri-Love: Living The Love Story Within You.*   shangri-love.com

My Inspired Thoughts

— *DAY 21* —

My Inspired Thoughts

— DAY 22 —

"If your Life isn't about the joy of it, something needs to change!

Do you want to lay on your death bed with regrets?

Address now issues that might otherwise become regrets, give yourself the gift of saying goodbye with a peaceful mind: Have the courage to be in integrity with yourself, and in doing so you will discover stupendous inner joy and freedom.

Life is a magical adventure that is meant to be enjoyed!"

Olivia DeMoss, Coach, Speaker, Peace Ambassador, Catalyst for Change, is on a mission to help push humanity forward, in service to our gorgeous Planet.   LivingTheLifeILove.net

My Inspired Thoughts

My Inspired Thoughts

"When we discover our passion, we find our purpose. Passion and purpose work together, igniting our inner light flame, radiating love. We are not alone on this journey. The people we meet along the way, in person, via ...books, media, movies, art, music, who embrace their passion, are our missing pieces. By doing what they love, following their hearts and inner light nudges, they ignite our passion, and in turn, inspire us to new heights. "

Rita Koivunen is a #1 International Best-Selling, Award-Winning Author, Inspirational Award-Winning and Published Artist, Colour Therapist and Therapeutic Watercolour Workshop Facilitator.   RitaKoivunen.com

My Inspired Thoughts

— _DAY 23_ —

My Inspired Thoughts

— *DAY 24* —

"Look Down Here! ~ How many people do you know with disabilities? The disabled are everywhere. We are among your co-workers, family, even at your Thanksgiving table. People with disabilities come in various sizes, shapes, colors, and attitudes—just like everyone else.

Today, and tomorrow, look me in the eye and converse with me. Engage with a gimp, and discover that there's NO difference. Let's change the world, one disabled person at a time!"

Suzanne Gorrell is a Disability Services expert and holds a B.S. in Disability Services from Southern Illinois University and is past President of the Partnership for Disability Issues. zortis1612@yahoo.com

My Inspired Thoughts

My Inspired Thoughts

*"You **are** the missing puzzle piece!!!*

Move from "ME TOO" (one of the crowd) to "ME ONLY" (the expert in your field).

Be the expert you were meant to be and let others be the experts they were meant to be and the puzzle will be complete!

You can't help everyone; "Choose One Avatar."

You can't do everything; "Solve One Problem."

Focus on the "Rule of ONE" and see amazing results!!!"

Daniel Hanzelka shows visionary entrepreneurs how to become "ME ONLY" experts, by putting together frameworks and systems to help them scale their business to the next level. ResetYourMoney.com

My Inspired Thoughts

My Inspired Thoughts

"The quality of your thoughts equals the quality of your life. When you start talking about what you want—instead of what you don't want—you set direction for your brain to get it done. I don't want to be poor is very different from I want to be rich in all areas of my life. The more vivid the picture and the more feeling you attach to it, the more you will achieve it."

Kalliope Barlis, the Phobia Relief Expert, Bestselling Author, Thought Leader utilizing Neuro-Linguistic Programming skills, helping thousands of people become better individuals—parents, spouses and workers.
ask@BuildingYourBest.com

My Inspired Thoughts

— *DAY 26* —

My Inspired Thoughts

"You are a beautiful soul with gifts to share with the world that are unique to you. As you journal each day, remember to clear your mind and open your heart. A divine power will emerge. Trust yourself and your words. Believe in the magic of YOU!"

Giselle Shapiro is a Visionary, Best-Selling Author, Midlife Women's Advocate, Speaker, Lifestyle Transformation Expert and Founder of LiteraryLaunch.com, an online global community for midlife women.

My Inspired Thoughts

— _DAY 27_ —

My Inspired Thoughts

"We are here to complete our life's purpose through finding our passion. Passion is a marriage of you, your creator and your creation. Whether you are passionate about artworks, words or music, the goal is the same: To find your purpose through your passion and fulfill a global purpose to achieve peace and harmony on earth. Finding the missing piece within allows you to complete life's mosaic in this world."

Jaz Gill is a poet and lyricist. Her poetry is in six anthologies, including three International Peace anthologies. Jaz instills peace and healing through her words. JazGill.com

My Inspired Thoughts

— _DAY 28_ —

My Inspired Thoughts

"'Life - 80% is just showing up'
        ~ Woody Allen

The other 20%? WASTED. Be all in! Give 100% in all you do!

We all know people who've either lost their passion or never had any! Less than just showing up! Sad.

You don't want to have any regrets when the time for that final transition... No one has said 'I wish I spent more time at work.'

Doing... not just thinking. Play at 100%!"

Marcia Merrill, aka "Transition Chick," is a Transformation Strategist, Life Transitions/Career Coach, Speaker, Trainer and Author of *Turning Midlife into the RIGHT Life!* 3StepTransitionCycle.com, MidLifeTransitionCoaching.com

My Inspired Thoughts

— *DAY 29* —

My Inspired Thoughts

"Words are powerful – they can express undying love, or shatter a soul. They can offer hope to the forlorn, or destroy a life without shedding even one drop of blood. Words can break a heart, or mend one; obliterate someone's confidence, or restore it. As a balm, words can soothe even the deepest wounds. As a weapon, damage inflicted by words might never heal. Be careful choosing your words – make sure they match your intentions."

Lily-Ann MacDonald is an award-winning writer, author, and editor with her company, Write-Rightly Full Service Editing and Writing Agency. Write-Rightly.com

My Inspired Thoughts

— *DAY 30* —

My Inspired Thoughts

— DAY 31 —

"Whenever you find yourself drawn to – maybe even obsessed with – something or someone, that's usually an indication of something inside yourself that wants to come out.

Let go of what other people tell you that you 'should' be doing and follow the guidance of your heart. The world eagerly awaits the unique contribution that only you can make.

Have faith, spread your wings, and fly."

Rachel S. Heslin is a Transformational Author and Speaker, and Founder of The Fullness of Your Power, inviting you to release your fears and step into your glory.
theFullnessofYourPower.com

My Inspired Thoughts

— *DAY 31* —

My Inspired Thoughts

"After losing most of my sight and having my life turned upside down, it has not kept me down. I have always been an optimistic person and I believe that your mindset is important when facing challenges.

Believe you can do it, picture it in your mind and make a plan. Once you have those 3 things then go for your dreams. Always know that you are a star no matter what anyone tells you!"

Yvonne Garris, the Fresh Outlook Coach, is on a mission to empower people with disabilities and help the newly disabled realize their lives have not ended.
Yvonne@FreshOutlookCoach.com

My Inspired Thoughts

— _DAY 32_ —

My Inspired Thoughts

"You need to be crystal clear on what you truly desire, have faith and believe it will happen in perfect divine timing. You need to leave the how up to the Universe and your Angels and you need to take inspired action.

You have the power to co-create the life and business that you truly desire. You are worthy of living an happy, fulfilled and abundant life. It is your time so GO for IT!"

Patricia LeBlanc is an Award-Winning Author, Master Energy Healer/Teacher, and Manifesting Expert. Patricia can help you create the life that you truly desire.
LoaLifeCoaching.com

My Inspired Thoughts

— _DAY_ 33 —

My Inspired Thoughts

"Being Highly Sensitive is a gift and a promise of power and magic:

• *It is a gift because it allows us to live deep and well-examined lives.*
• *It is a promise because we use it to make positive changes in the world, small and large, inner and outer.*
• *It is power because it gives us deep and accurate insights.*
• *It is magic because it allows us to see patterns and experience life multi-dimensionally."*

Gitte Lassen, the Positive Power Pilgrim, helps Highly Sensitive People transform from being painfully, vulnerable sensitive to being confidently, powerfully sensitive. GitteLassen.com

My Inspired Thoughts

— _DAY 34_ —

My Inspired Thoughts

"When the going gets tough, just breathe in and out
Focus on your breath, that's enough.
When times get rough, just take one step
One after another, that's enough.
When fear grips, you just talk to it
One word at a time, that's enough.
When nothing helps, just hang in there.
Breath after breath, step after step
Word following word, one step at a time.
You will see light!"

Disability and chronic illness has taught **Bianka Brankovic** about life's challenges. Bianka empowers others through coaching, writing and speaking. Her message centers around never giving up. facebook.com/DisabledWomenMessage

My Inspired Thoughts

— _DAY_ 35 —

My Inspired Thoughts

"There is no such thing like a "natural born" mom. Every woman has to learn what it means to be a mother and how to cope with the new situation in life. So don't be afraid to ask for help and look for someone who can give you a hand with your child. Seeking advice and being ready to learn is the real meaning of being a good mom."

Anja Riemer-Grobe, Founder of "Joyful Mom," the community for happy moms who love their family life and enjoy being a mom.   Anja-Riemer.de (German only) or Anja@Anja-Riemer.de (English)

My Inspired Thoughts

My Inspired Thoughts

"Through Pop Art, the movies, music television shows, and cartoons that brought joy and laughter to millions can be expressed again.

Every color, brush stroke, or pencil to paper/canvas can bring your childhood dreams and fond memories to life.

Extract your happiest, fondest memories by doodling things that bring to you the greatest pleasures in pop culture. This will then transmute pain, sorrow or depression from the darkness to the light."

Gabriel R. Gonzalez is a native Brooklyn, New York free-lance Graphic Artist and Art Specialist teaching to special needs adults, as well as children.
facebook.com/gabriel.gonzalez.14019

My Inspired Thoughts

— _DAY 37_ —

My Inspired Thoughts

"Communicating with Universal Wisdom has proven to be a powerful resource for me over the past few years.

By doing so, I wrote my book, Soul Destiny Discovery *and produced my Multi Media workshop against phenomenal odds. My resource was my spiritual boardroom where I invited, listened to and acted on guidance from many entities long gone. I now communicate through Akashic records and my spiritual guides.*

Learn to do this and access unrestricted Universal talent and wisdom."

Phil Ross, Best-Selling Author of *Soul Destiny Discovery* and producer of the now internationally expanding Mastery Development Group and Soul Destiny progressive transformation workshops.   MasteryDevelopmentGroup.com

My Inspired Thoughts

My Inspired Thoughts

"My story begins when I was a little five-year-old girl, believing everything was great in my world, then shortly, woke up to discover myself in a refugee camp, escaping from war.

My journey's wisdom: We need to put effort into finding inspiration while we start our new lives. Your role models may be different; you'll need to find help along your personal path to success. Fill your own journey to success with love, peace and positivity!"

Phouphet Chounramany is a National Vice President for the Freedom Equity Group, Best-Selling Author, emerging Leader in network marketing, Life Coach, and stay-at-home Mom.   Phouphet@PhouphetChounramany.com

My Inspired Thoughts

— _DAY 39_ —

My Inspired Thoughts

"Brighten Your Day with Turquoise to Relieve Mental Illness Symptoms. My angels gave me a mission to speak out about mental illness. Their message: If someone uses turquoise in their daily lives, it will soothe them and get them through their day.

Let's support people with depression, anxiety, etc. It is OK to acknowledge your suffering. It is a stepping stone to a journey of healing and leading a happier, more interactive and fulfilled life."

Catherine M. Laub is a Best-Selling Author, Speaker, Radio Show Host, Psychic-Medium, Spiritual Guide, Workshop Facilitator, Wife, Mother, and Grandmother. CatherineMLaub.com

My Inspired Thoughts

— *DAY 40* —

My Inspired Thoughts

"What gifts and talents do you possess that you can use to make this world a better place? To enrich not only your own life, but the lives of countless other people all around you.

You see, the same light shines in your soul as it does in everyone else on this planet. Inspire others and let your light shine out to everyone. Don't be afraid to be who you are truly meant to be."

Susan Anderson O'Brien is a Reiki Healer, Nurse, Angel Intuitive, Digital Marketer and Author of *Crystal Magic - Discover The Power Of Crystals.* SuesHealingRays.com

My Inspired Thoughts

My Inspired Thoughts

— DAY 42 —

*"A **WorkJockey** is someone who places life ahead of work. You work to live; you don't live to work. Someone else once uttered those words many years ago. That premise is as true today, if not even more relevant to the kind of life you wish to lead. You have different needs, desires, goals, and dreams. However, we all share a common aim, obtaining an income is a necessity to live a normal, prosperous life."*

Sam Slay, SPHR, SHRM-SCP, is a Speaker, Leadership Trainer, HR Coach, Facilitator, Author of the Bestseller *WorkJockey* and Retired Chief of Police with 24 years experience. SamSlay.com

My Inspired Thoughts

My Inspired Thoughts

"'Be the Difference' Leaders share (3) characteristics globally: They Live Beyond their Circumstances; Advocate for Themselves and Others; and are Abundant Life Ambassadors.

These 'Be the Difference' leadership traits show up in your ability to use your gifts for the greater good, negotiate with success, and appreciate the cherished life you're creating.

This framework will help you make a profit and create a meaningful difference in the world."

Corine Wofford, CEO, Certified Master Facilitator and Best-Selling Author, speaks globally on Negotiation and Leadership, mentoring corporate leaders and women entrepreneurs worldwide to Be the Difference.   CorineWofford.com

My Inspired Thoughts

_____

_____

_____

_____

_____

_____

_____

_____

_____

_____

_____

_____

_____

_____

_____

_____

_____

— _DAY 43_ —

My Inspired Thoughts

"Connection ― we either yearn for it or shrink away in solitude. Shadowed or visible, we're complete parts of the bigger picture ... self-sustaining and yet dependent upon each other for survival.

Apart from differences ― and in light of them ― humankind dazzles with diversity. The loudest voices mingle to characterize us, providing an incomplete definition of our essence while many sweet sounds lie dormant. Aware of their absence, we're fractured. Are _you_ the missing piece?"

Judith Cassis, C.Ht., Book coach, 2013 _New York Times/LA Times_ Bestselling ghostwriter, Founder of Writers Mastermind Alliance™ and WritertoWriterSuccessAcademy.com, and Keynote Speaker. JudithCassis.com

My Inspired Thoughts

— DAY 44 —

My Inspired Thoughts

"You were born for this time to bring your vibrancy, love, talent, faith, hope and presence to every interaction at work, with friends, family and in the community.

Become visible, avoid disappearing, shrinking, or fading away in this time of increasing intolerance, hatred, fear and distress.

You are so desperately needed in our world. Come, pour out your hope, encouragement, kindness, compassion and calm every day. A little influence can bring someone refreshing peace."

Ruth Littler is a Strategic Intervention Coach and Counsellor at Brilliant Living. BrillantLiving.net.au

My Inspired Thoughts

My Inspired Thoughts

"Authenticity is the New Audacity! Have you ever heard this phrase: "It's nothing personal, it's just business"? I have. Every time I hear it, it still disappoints me. Today, business is personal and people do business with ME because of ME.

And, they should do business with YOU because of YOU. Not because you perfected some persuasive presentation or recently attended a sales seminar on how to over-come someone's objections. It's because you've tapped into the true you."

TR Garland, Wall Street Journal® Award Winner in Field of Business, #1 Best-Selling Author, Speaker, Coaching Industry Veteran & Insider, and Creator of 3-Step LinkedIn Success System. LinkedInSpecialReport.com

My Inspired Thoughts

— *DAY 46* —

My Inspired Thoughts

"Making Success Inevitable ~ Plan backwards. Focus only on what will move you towards your vision. Your future success is based on what you do today. Having a vision is the first step. When you can break down the steps of the vision to daily habits and practices to 15 minutes daily, your success is inevitable. Day by day as you move nearer towards your goals, your habits keep you on the track of success."

Dr. Sundardas D. Annamalay is CEO of NTC Alliance Group of Companies, Amazon Best-Selling Author, Award-Winning Entrepreneur, Professor of Natural Medicine, and a Naturopathic Physician. theFreedom-Formula.com

My Inspired Thoughts

— *DAY 47* —

My Inspired Thoughts

— *DAY 48* —

"At some point or the other, we all experience tough times. It's your call how you wish to approach the situation. Why not make yours an empowering one with the right frame of mind?

A positive frame of mind makes a hurdle appear like a challenge to be won. It's your Hero's Journey providing an opportunity to learn, grow and emerge stronger with the gift of knowledge to help others caught in a similar situation."

Vatsala Shukla is a Career & Business Coach, Author and Change Catalyst for professionals who want to achieve their career aspirations with life balance. KarmicAllyCoaching.com

My Inspired Thoughts

— _DAY 48_ —

My Inspired Thoughts

"Make Your Personal Essence Your Personal Presence!

Going inwards before any presentation and making contact with your Higher Self – your True Essence – will connect you with your audience from the start. When you show that part of you not conditioned from childhood and with no limitations, you immediately bond with the fundamental nature of others. You are connecting your humanness making others remember where they really come from, and you will reach a Spiritual Rapport with your audience."

Juracy Johnson is a Best-Selling Author, Speaker, Coach and Founder of "Proyecto M", a Guided System for Latin American Women who want to create their success. www.Juracy.com

My Inspired Thoughts

— *DAY 49* —

My Inspired Thoughts

— *DAY 50* —

"You are dead. Your immortal spirit separates from your physical body. You look down wondering what existence will be like without your body. You look up and realize you no longer feel the pains of mortality. You are free of the temporal effects of sneezing, sickness, and silly emotions. You still remember everything, but now, you remember <u>everything</u>!

What memories are you creating right now? Life is good. Look to God. Things will work out."

Kyle LB Morey is an Award-Winning, International Best-Selling Author, Speaker, and father of the *furious five*. Currently wandering the planet as a world-schooling parent. <u>KyleLBMorey.com</u>

My Inspired Thoughts

My Inspired Thoughts

— *DAY 51* —

"The Power of Wishes ~ Longing for more freedom in life, a job you love or travelling the world?

Like the sun and rain makes a seed in the soil grow into a flower, make good wishes for others in your thoughts and actions.

This way you fill your mind with good impressions and develop a lasting feeling of inner wealth and richness on all levels. Then your wishes will manifest on the outside."

Jette Bilberg Lauritsen is a 2 times International Best-Selling Author, and a Health and Wealth Coach.
www.jettebl.dk

My Inspired Thoughts

— *DAY 51* —

My Inspired Thoughts

"We all deserve to be successful and to live the DREAM life. The question is: How do you get it all? I am a strong believer that EVERYONE is born with a special skill set and talent to be prosperous and great at something they feel passionate about! You just have to find that passion and activate your 'dream mode' setting to live the life you always wanted. Never stop believing and push hard for your goals!"

Katia KITA, International Best-Selling Author, Public Figure and Speaker, and Creator of Get.Reinvented™ online fitness series. <u>ImagineNewYou.com</u>

My Inspired Thoughts

— <u>DAY 52</u> —

My Inspired Thoughts

"There's no shame in feeling angry. All big feelings have a secret message. Thanks to Dr. Becky Bailey, founder of Conscious Discipline®, today I know anger says, 'calm down and change.' When you know the four roots of anger (protection, unfair, change, and stress), you can calm down and choose your next best move. Breathe. Tell yourself, 'I am safe. I am loved. I can handle this.' Anger is just the messenger. You are the boss."

Nancy Lucas, M.Ed., CDCI is Mama of 4, "Be a Nice Mom" podcast host, and helps frustrated moms prevent meltdowns, handle outbursts and get their kids to cooperate.
Nancy@BeaNiceMom.com

My Inspired Thoughts

My Inspired Thoughts

— *DAY 54* —

"The most significant 'Aha' is realizing that life doesn't happen 'To' you, it happens 'For' you. There's wisdom to be mined from every experience, whether windfall or wound. Asking: Truth: If X happened/is happening for my highest and best, what might that be? provides personal choice regarding the gifts to extract from any experience. What if embracing this awareness is the missing element in being open to the infinite possibilities which are available to you?"

Maureen Marie Damery, Self-Empowerment Facilitator, Author of the book/workshop, *Your Owner's Manual For Life ~ Source Code of Your Soul*, former Microsoft software engineer. MaureenDamery.com

My Inspired Thoughts

— _DAY 54_ —

My Inspired Thoughts

"Compassion and gratitude are feelings we all benefit by reaching for on a regular basis in life. When you come at things from a place of compassion you will find it easier to accept, understand and support yourself and others. Gratitude allows you to tune in to all the beautiful desires you have requested from the Universe so you can receive them in abundance and feel great in the process. Simple, but rarely easy!"

Debbie Pokornik is a green tea enthusiast, award-winning author and radio host whose mission is to help everyday women create extraordinary lives.   EmpoweringNRG.com

My Inspired Thoughts

— _DAY 55_ —

My Inspired Thoughts

_____
_____
_____
_____
_____
_____
_____
_____
_____
_____
_____
_____
_____
_____
_____
_____
_____
_____
_____
_____
_____
_____
_____
_____
_____
_____
_____
_____
_____

"Life is a series of dreams carefully thought; ideas are actions which have to be exceptionally implemented. Friendship is the energy that helps us drive while love is the way that inspires the heart. In all, life can be wonderful but it is your own decision. You grow and prosper; influence and inspire; bring life and joy. Just be positive and an optimist. Believe in what you want to accomplish and find your beautiful life."

Luis Vicente Garcia is a Business Performance Coach, Speaker, Best-Selling Author, Goodwill and Entrepreneurship Ambassador, focusing on goals, motivation and leadership. @LVGarciaG

My Inspired Thoughts

— _DAY 56_ —

My Inspired Thoughts

"Make Each Day a Sun-day! ~ There is a YOU beyond the everyday you, free of all fear. This Higher 'I/Eye' lives in/around your whole body. When you are in 'the zone,' you are in full contact and expression of this Higher Self. Time and space cease. Creativity pours in.

To instantly ignite this flow, imagine from your chest, a brilliant sun expanding open. Trust and tap this center over your thymus. Inhale inspiration streaming in from beyond your everyday mind."

Lisa Loving Dalton is a Best-Selling Author, Actor, Stunt-woman in 200+ Films, TV and Commercials, John Maxwell Certified, Inspirational Speaker and a Michael Chekhov Master. LisaDalton.com

My Inspired Thoughts

— _DAY 57_ —

My Inspired Thoughts

"One way to succeed in life ~ I once visited a used car lot to buy a vehicle. The lot had 18 white cars and one red car. I grabbed my pencil and jotted down my observation. The red car stood out above all the white ones. From this, I tell my family, friends and clients about life... 'Always BE the red car.' In other words, always be DIFFERENT and always STAND OUT!"

Manny Carter is a #1 Best-Selling Author, Baby Boomer, Dating Expert, and Psychic. MannyCarter.com

My Inspired Thoughts

My Inspired Thoughts

"In life, you just need to make a decision to get going. Not making a decision is still making a decision. However, this does not move the needle towards accomplishing your goal. Start with baby steps. You will get to your destination. You can correct course along your path. Life throws curve balls. How you respond is what makes the difference. Remaining flexible and open is key to accomplishing what it is you want."

Matt Santi enjoys spending time with his family & friends. He is a proud Eagle Scout & go-getter. Personal motto: Sometimes the wait is worth it!   MattSanti.com

My Inspired Thoughts

My Inspired Thoughts

— _DAY 60_ —

"I've learnt that you can't control the situations that you are faced with, how ever much you steer, guide and hope.

There will be unforeseen and unwelcomed situations, which will leave you uncertain and confused.

What you do have power over is you. You have the power to engage intentionally, engage with conviction, engage with love, and most importantly to engage with life.

Take the opportunity and you'll find the solace and solutions for your way forward."

Jenny Garrett is an award-winning Coach, Author, Trainer and Speaker. She is Transforming the World for everyone, One Empowered Woman at a Time.   JennyGarrett.Global

My Inspired Thoughts

— *DAY 60* —

My Inspired Thoughts

— DAY 61 —

"Success will come to you by following this three-step process:
Visualize - *experience your dream in your mind as if it has already happened, then write it down.*
Strategize - *spend time designing plans necessary for achievement, find a mentor to help you.*
Energize - *take action on your plans with persistence and a sense of urgency.*
Celebrate your success and choose to live every day with joy!"

Maria Luchsinger, Best-Selling Author, Speaker, Founder of The Women's Career Transformation Network. A career strategist, she coaches women so they can find joy in balanced lives. MariaLuchsinger.com

My Inspired Thoughts

My Inspired Thoughts

— *DAY 62* —

"When I was 8 years old, I was sent to a mental institution for 3 years for a crime I didn't commit. I eventually proved my innocence, gained my freedom, and helped my family come together to heal. Now I travel the world sharing my story and the three biggest lessons I learned that will help you take your life to the next level: Love, Forgive, Never Give Up."

Bill Hargenrader, The Next Level Coach, is a Best-Selling Author, International Speaker, Founder of True You Solutions, Successful Online Summit Systems, and Next Level Life. NextLevelLife.net

My Inspired Thoughts

My Inspired Thoughts

— DAY 63 —

"Your Legacy of Peace ~ One way is to build your mindset so you oscillate in high, positive, peaceful awakened states of mind. Practice catching yourself judging, gossiping or being negative and stop it. Transform your words to high vibrational words, which are supportive and solution orientated, that expand you, not contract, drain and stress you and others. It's a choice. You will create better relationships, better outcomes, be healthier and leave peaceful footsteps in your world and our world."

Bernadette Dimitrov, aka Australia's 1st official Mrs Claus, is a Happiness and Peace Ambassador, Best-Selling Author, Trainer and Founder of <u>SantaClausPeaceSchool.com</u>.

My Inspired Thoughts

My Inspired Thoughts

"One of the immediate challenges in learning to read is dealing with the complex sound/spelling relationship in words. The Color-Coded Reading system fixes the many basic literacy problems with the regulated sound/spelling educational resources and teaching strategy to achieving successful and proficient readers fast. The color-coded regulated sound/spelling system is the new super-highway to literacy success."

Margaret Chen, Originator of Color-Coded Reading System; Discoverer of the Sound/Spelling Relationship Theorem, Developer of RiC Teaching Methodology, and Designer of Reading in Color (RiC) Educational Resources.
facebook.com/ReadingInColour

My Inspired Thoughts

— *DAY 64* —

My Inspired Thoughts

"How often does a person look at the positive aspects in their life with appreciation? Many are not leveraging the full power of positive momentum available to them. These moments reassure us and remind us that we can create a personal reality that we are truly happy with. Many people are reaching for this place, but need assistance. It is possible to trust the process of one's unique life while happily expanding into new experiences."

Sharonda Thomas is an uplifting writer, designer, musician and a natural teacher with a unique personal perspective and knows how to relay this to others.
TrusttheProcess.wixsite.com/TrusttheProcess

My Inspired Thoughts

— _DAY 65_ —

My Inspired Thoughts

"Burnout is no stranger to those in Healthcare. The characteristics that draw us to care for others leave us vulnerable to not leaving enough for ourselves. We must learn to turn that around. Journaling is one tool to renew our spirit. Keeping a gratitude journal allows us to see our many blessings and to feel our abundance. And gratitude is contagious. The more we acknowledge our abundance, the more our lives are fulfilled."

Debra Croy, Nursing Professional, Speaker, Journal Maker - working to support healthcare quality, patient/staff safety improvements and community health. Helping you be a better you! Croylnc@cox.net

My Inspired Thoughts

— _DAY 66_ —

My Inspired Thoughts

— _DAY 67_ —

"Holding curiosity and compassion for yourself opens a door to your soul that would otherwise remain closed. By creating an environment within you based on compassionate curiosity, you can go deeper within and enter a space of acceptance and healing, allowing the neglected child within you to express herself.

Try to treat yourself with as much compassion as you would a neglected child. After all, you're doing the best you can."

Teresa Dawn Abram, Registered Health Coach, Certified Holistic Wellness Coach, Speaker, Believer in personal power, and Founder of PurpleDoorHealth.ca.

My Inspired Thoughts

— _DAY 67_ —

My Inspired Thoughts

— DAY 68 —

"What if the answers you've been looking for were already inside you?

What if it was easy to bring fun, purpose, impact to your business and life?

You know there's MORE to life than money... there are uncharted territories to explore.

Maybe you've been playing safe or putting other people's priorities first.

I challenge you to explore new possibilities, where the limits to what you can achieve are only the ones YOU set on yourself."

Clara Noble is a best-selling author, and a passionate mentor empowering conscious entrepreneurs to live their dreams, find their Unique Genius, make money and communicate powerfully.   Clara@YourUniqueGenius.com

My Inspired Thoughts

My Inspired Thoughts

— *DAY 69* —

"Never be afraid to ask 'why'. 'Why' can change the world. 'Why' can help you grow. 'Why' can be the difference between doing the wrong thing and doing the right thing. Understanding the 'why' gives you more insight than you ever thought possible. I truly believe that adults with a childlike need to know 'why' are the most successful and the most fulfilled. Never be afraid to ask 'why'."

Tamica Sears is a Leadership Development Coach currently residing in sunny Arizona. Look for her upcoming book, *How to Tell if you're an A$$hole Manager.*   SearsCoaching.com

My Inspired Thoughts

My Inspired Thoughts

"There's magic in your smile. Forgive me if I stare at it for awhile. . .

May God grant you always a sunbeam to warm you, a moonbeam to charm you, a sheltering Angel so nothing can harm you. Laughter to cheer you. Faithful friends near you. And whenever you pray, Heaven to hear you."

Ashley Kayson is a Student Mentor at CareerVillage.org, Depression & Bipolar Support Alliance Ambassador, American Foundation For Suicide Prevention Advocate, and College student at Ashworth Online College.
alkayson@mymail.aacc.edu

My Inspired Thoughts

— DAY 70 —

My Inspired Thoughts

— DAY 71 —

"Belief in yourself - in essence a strong sense of self-worth, self-esteem and self-confidence - is the foundational key to success. The key to developing an unshakable self-assurance is the ability to release anger and forgive yourself and others. Without this ability practiced regularly, you will self-sabotage and never reach your full potential. Free yourself from the burden of unforgiveness starting now. Release oppressive negative emotions, practice daily gratitude, and begin living the life you deserve today."

Carma Spence is an Author, Award-winning Speaker, Coach, and Creative Genius helping women release self-doubt and create profitable information products around their (sometimes obscure) hobbies. CarmaSpence.com

My Inspired Thoughts

— _DAY 71_ —

My Inspired Thoughts

— DAY 72 —

"Why is getting started so difficult?
- It is easy to romanticize the outcome when it is solely in your mind.
- There are no failures yet.
How to get started?
- Break it down into bite-sized pieces - write them down.
- Do the easiest/quickest one first - just to gain momentum.
- Do the hardest one next - to get it out of the way.
- Stay focused as you are doing each step by minimizing distractions.
- Finished."

Virlane Torbit is an International Speaker, Canfield Success Principles Trainer, Life Coach, and Retreat Host in Phuket, Thailand. SpeakerVirlane@gmail.com

My Inspired Thoughts

My Inspired Thoughts

— DAY 73 —

"Retirement should not be thought of as an end, nor is it a beginning. Treating it as such is a mistake. Retirement should be viewed as just another step in your journey. How long it lasts is unknown, but how far you'll go depends on how well you've planned. Find your path, tread cautiously, and map out any hidden dangers along the way. For one small misstep today can greatly impact all of your tomorrows."

Tom Alessi is a Nationally Recognized Authority on 401(k), 403(b) and Other Group Retirement Plans and President of Westwood Wealth Advisors. <u>Westwood-Wealth.com</u>

My Inspired Thoughts

— *DAY 73* —

My Inspired Thoughts

"Lead with Your Divine Feminine energy, which **holds the keys** to your purpose, your mission, your right tribe. She taps into the unlimited abundance of Source to create solutions that never existed before.

*Follow with Your Divine Masculine that **fleshes out a plan**, with implementation strategies, dates and action items.*

First your feminine dreams the idea, then your masculine can act. You must have both, in that order, for sustainable success."

Julie Foucht, Art of Feminine Marketing, teaches female coaches, teachers and healers who are frustrated with traditional marketing, how to build 6-figure businesses that honor their feminine essence. JulieFoucht.com

My Inspired Thoughts

— DAY 74 —

My Inspired Thoughts

"Don't worry about failure; everyone fails.

Ignore the naysayers, because when most people fail they give up; instead of dusting themselves off and moving forward. Some of them then make it their life's mission to spread their failure and misery to all the visionaries they encounter.

Instead focus on the things that are true, honorable, innocent, modest, friendly, or reputable. Esteem valor and things that are commendable, everything else is a distraction or an excuse."

William Shea is Founder and Senior Pastor of The Ekklesian House, a church with its focus on fellowship and home scripture study instead of lecture. WilliamShea.org

My Inspired Thoughts

— _DAY 75_ —

My Inspired Thoughts

"You are worthy and full of value. Each person has something unique to share. Connect within to find that seed of potential and nurture it to let it grow. Don't let fears and the judgement of others deter you and release those limiting beliefs holding you back. Follow the path that feels the lightest and right for you and your purpose will unfold. Claim your power and stand up and share it with the world."

Wanda Davis, M.Sc., B.Sc., B.Ed., aka The Power Shifter, is a Certified Coach/Energy Conductor, Reiki Master/Teacher, Access Consciousness® Bars Facilitator, Shamanic Practitioner, Author and Speaker. WandaDavis.ca

My Inspired Thoughts

— _DAY 76_ —

My Inspired Thoughts

— DAY 77 —

"There's a simple weapon in the fight against failing at a task. I call it the SHIELD OF BELIEF. When you BELIEVE in a particular goal, you can put forward your best effort. When you BELIEVE you have the right action plan in place, you can focus on the end result. And when you surround yourself with positivity, you can BELIEVE your efforts will end in success.

All you need to do is BELIEVE."

Donna L Martin, Kidlit Author of *The Story Catcher*, Creator of *Book Nook Reviews*, Host of *Writerly Wisdom*, Book Reviewer for Harper Collins, and SCBWI member. DonnaLMartin.com

My Inspired Thoughts

— DAY 77 —

My Inspired Thoughts

— DAY 78 —

"In order to receive love, we must give love out unto the world. Write sticky notes with love statements. Stick them to anything tangible in your path such as trees, buildings, etc. The wind will blow these notes away onto other tangible things. A second form of love is appreciation. Write thank you notes with appreciative statements to everyone you know. A promotion, new love, or surprise will be the result. Give Love to Get Love!"

Shirley Jusino is an Int'l #1 Best-Selling co-author of *Ready, Aim, Thrive!* and *My Big Idea Book,* Winner of two Gold eLit awards for Literacy Excellence. ShirleyJusino@ymail.com

My Inspired Thoughts

— DAY 78 —

My Inspired Thoughts

"To THRIVE rather than just survive is one of the most important mind shifts that we can make.

When we truly understand and live the paradigm that our 'Health IS our Wealth' we can then start to redefine success to be based on the inclusion of our mind, body and Spirit health as part of our daily work priorities.

As a result we can have a much more nourishing experience of our work and life."

Wendy Dumaresq is an Author, Speaker, Women's Health Practitioner, Business Consultant, Event Facilitator, and Founder of THRIVE for Women Leaders.
RadiantWomenBook.com

My Inspired Thoughts

— *DAY 79* —

My Inspired Thoughts

"I have spent much of my adult life picking up the missing pieces of myself that I lost through a traumatic childhood. I have grown to realize that each person's life is encouraging this pursuit, whether through acts of nature, relationship problems, or health issues. We are also being urged to add our ever-increasing piece to every situation we encounter. When we notice that something is missing, the first question should be, 'Is it I?'"

Anne Redelfs, MD is a retired psychiatrist who lives in Texarkana, TX. She practices deep listening – hearing souls relay what they need for their development.
AnneTheListener.com

My Inspired Thoughts

— _DAY 80_ —

My Inspired Thoughts

— DAY 81 —

"Rise to a place of higher perspective to achieve greater personal balance physically, mentally, emotionally and spiritually. In this extremely beneficial process, you'll awaken that wonderful catalyst, YOU, to share your gifts and talents with the world. It is in this place of heartfelt gratefulness and health, that you gain increased clarity in purpose and are moved to encourage positive transformations in others. Know YOU ARE that unique missing piece! Are you up for it?"

Susanne Morrone is a Best-Selling Author, Speaker, and Distinguished Natural Health Coach. She shares targeted, practical wisdom to achieve health on a shortened learning curve. NaturalHealthChat.com

My Inspired Thoughts

— *DAY 81* —

My Inspired Thoughts

"Stay alert to the world around you. Keep your guard up and don't get distracted from your goals and responsibilities. There are a lot of people who are ready to take advantage of any weakness you show. You don't want to end up being taken in by a con or a scam. Use your head, stay in the moment, and you will be well ahead of the game in living a scam-free life."

Joe Libby, International Speaker and Entertainer from San Antonio, TX. Joe utilizes his expert knowledge of magic and deception to educate on the dangers of cons and scams. JoeLibbySeminars.com   (Photo by Jacklen Taylor at Outlaw Photography)

My Inspired Thoughts

My Inspired Thoughts

"Some women reach 50 and believe that their useful life is over. Other women reach 50 and believe that this is the start of a whole new exciting phase of their life when they can truly start to live for themselves. Guess which group lives longer and has the best time?

There is a growing trend for women at midlife to become entrepreneurs. They are ready to pursue their dream and live their purpose."

Pat Duckworth is a Midlife Mentor, Author, and Int'l Public Speaker. She is passionate about inspiring women to live their best lives, regardless of their age.
HotWomenCoolSolutions.com

My Inspired Thoughts

— *DAY 83* —

My Inspired Thoughts

"'They say that, when the student is ready, the teacher appears. The truth is that the teacher was always there; the student was just not ready to see her.'

'Never achieve a goal without first having its replacement.'

'Friends do not count the favors sought in the pleasure of the giving.'

'Your Best Friend accepts you as you are; your Mentor wants you to be all you can be.'"

Nick Arden, Life and Career Coach, uses his 5 decades of experience and 14 careers to help clients cope with technology's impact on job markets.
Nick@TechImpact-Coaching.com

My Inspired Thoughts

— _DAY 84_ —

My Inspired Thoughts

"Successful people use the tool of persistence to weather every storm. It starts with visualizing the goal and being so connected to it that nothing will stop you. Then every morning, when they have the most energy and focus, they work on their most difficult tasks. People who start each day by tackling their challenges are energized by their accomplishments and sail through the rest of the day towards their final goal with less stress."

Bill McCarthy is president of Unity Foundation, producer of the annual Peace Day Global Broadcast and producer and host of the Positive Spin Television Program. UnityFoundation.org

My Inspired Thoughts

— DAY 85 —

My Inspired Thoughts

"'Those who tell the stories rule the world.' - Hopi American Indian proverb

We all have unique stories inside us and few leadership opportunities are more powerful than when you 'tell me a story.' Facts and figures are important, but nothing touches hearts, influences decisions and changes minds like great storytelling. Fascinating stories can be written, spoken or visual, but the storyteller's secret is to always make your audience feel something. What story will you tell today?"

Janet Vasil is a Media Trainer, Brand Journalist, Speaker and Author, and Founder of Vasil Media Group | Your Media Moment & Beyond training and consulting. VasilMediaGroup.com

My Inspired Thoughts

— DAY 86 —

My Inspired Thoughts

"Those who have experienced a significant degree of success - in any field - have dared to put their own brand on it! You've got to have your own unique identity; otherwise you're just another wannabe. Discover what you do best, and then either become the best at doing it or figure out how to do it well but in a unique way. You'll be light years ahead of your competitors in the quest for lasting success."

Stephen Boutelle, The Premiere Info-Strategist, teaches his clients how to create their OWN Brand of Success, Marketing Consultant, co-created products with top marketers, and co-founder of IMNewswatch.com.   prosperityunleashed.com

My Inspired Thoughts

— _DAY 87_ —

My Inspired Thoughts

— *DAY 88* —

*"Scientists have shown everything is **ENERGY** and it cannot be created or destroyed, only transformed. Which means you, the food you eat, clothes you wear, technology you use as well as your thoughts, feelings, and emotions are all energy. In Quantum Physics and the double slit experiment, electrons act randomly until an observer is present. The observer is you my friend and your life is not random."*

"You ARE the one creating your reality!"

Susan Shatzer, a 6 time #1 Int'l Best-Selling Author, TV/ Radio guest, Speaker, Facilitator, and Single Mom, who can help you finally feel GOOD ENOUGH!   SusanShatzer.com

My Inspired Thoughts

— _DAY 88_ —

My Inspired Thoughts

"I can't remember a time when I wasn't a helper. Being a helper is a good thing, in moderation. Without renewing your own personal resources, there is less and less to give. So, what can a recovering helper teach you? Self-care first. Deep loving self-care. Self-care that feeds your soul and nurtures your spirit. What feeds you? What leaves you feeling alive, vibrant and filled with joy? Do more of that. Do it often."

Jerri Shankler, LCSW LCADC helps families step out of the addiction drama and get their lives back.
JerriShankler.com

My Inspired Thoughts

— *DAY 89* —

My Inspired Thoughts

"Live in the now, mindful of the beauty and success of every moment.

Play full out. Stop pretending that you are not great! Take the next step in your vision for the future. Regardless of how others behave or respond, take action anyway!

The world is abundant with opportunity, a deep well of aliveness. Don't just sip because you fear there's not enough. Drink fully and freely with gratitude! Remember, it is always your choice!"

Patricia Clason, Trainer since 1975, Emotional Intelligence Expert, Professional Speaker, and Coach. Her latest program, *Successful Living Basic Training* helps clients live on purpose and in prosperity. PatriciaClason.com

My Inspired Thoughts

— _DAY 90_ —

My Inspired Thoughts

— DAY 91 —

"Begin every day in a state of gratitude. Be grateful for everything you have received and all that is yet to come. Grant forgiveness to everyone who has harmed you. Discover your own inner peace. Be the beacon of light, hope and love humanity requires. Be the shining example for the world to see and follow.

Today you can do anything!

Let's save the planet one soul at a time, starting with your own!"

Marycarol Ross is The Spiritual Archaeologist, Author, Medical Intuitive, Speaker, Spiritual Healer, Medium, Life Coach, Career Intuitive, Mediator, and Master Intuitive. MarycarolRoss.com

My Inspired Thoughts

— _DAY 91_ —

My Inspired Thoughts

— DAY 92 —

"IT'S TIME TO TALK! Mental illnesses are as distressing as physical illnesses; BUT mental illness is invisible. The stigma attached leaves the vulnerable even more isolated and entrapped within themselves, with no escape route.

NO ONE IS EXEMPT!

Let us show love and compassion to ALL; a kind word, a smile, a helping hand can transform a life. It is strong to make yourself vulnerable, NOT weak: it gives others permission to be vulnerable too."

Margaret Reece, BA HONS, is a Trauma Coach and Author of upcoming book, *HOPE RESTORED, A Guide to Embracing the Storms of Developmental PTSD.*
MargaretReece2016@gmail.com

My Inspired Thoughts

— *DAY 92* —

My Inspired Thoughts

"Success is a journey, not a destination. It is realized by pursuing an ongoing series of progressively grander goals, each a land-mark from which to observe your progress, and there are many such beautiful vistas to enjoy along the way. The sooner you begin your journey, the sooner you can enjoy the view.

The secret to completing a marathon is believing you can take the next step."

Ken Jackson is a Shaman, Author, Speaker, Life Coach, Fitness Coach, and Founder of Build A Life Worth Dreaming. BuildaLifeWorthDreaming.com

My Inspired Thoughts

— _DAY 93_ —

My Inspired Thoughts

"Your soul has a plan, and it's messy! When you understand the 'mess' and pain that may accompany it, you gain the keys to your success!

We are all connected energetically and you are here on a personal and global mission! When you learn to use the pain of your challenges and seek to understand your soul's objectives, you free yourself. You are open to receive all you deserve: money, health, love, etcetera!"

Vicki Murphy, Integrative Energy Practitioner, Medium, Teacher, Author, Radio Personality, Creator of Angelically Spoken & Quantum Projection Tools for Healing and Rapid Manifesting. WestCoastMedium.com

My Inspired Thoughts

— _DAY 94_ —

My Inspired Thoughts

"Spirituality is not about 'doing' but about surrender. Surrender, universal component, without which no significant transformation and spiritual growth can occur. It is being willing to open our hearts to see blessings in every trial in life, to our True Self - within each of us, which it is attuned to wisdom, truth, beauty, and love.

The essence of the Power of Now: getting the most joy out of our journey, which makes life worth living."

Pedro Power is a Healer, Spiritual Guide, and Transformational Coach committed to remaining mindful of life as a mysterious, continued spiritual journey of healing and transformation. PedroPower.com

My Inspired Thoughts

— DAY 95 —

My Inspired Thoughts

"The most meaningful and often painful lessons in life have the underlying theme of 'when to keep pursuing your desire or when to let go and walk away.' If you are used to making ego-based decisions, your ego will lead you astray. Open up to your Higher Self who knows what direction is the best for you. Learn to trust your Higher Self. This is your key to wisdom, happiness and to your personal evolution."

Rev. Lynn Walker is a Metaphysics Teacher, Professional Astrologer, Speaker, Reiki Master and Author of the book series *Wisdom From Spirit Guides*. LiveConsciously.org 952-941-2321

My Inspired Thoughts

— _DAY 96_ —

My Inspired Thoughts

— DAY 97 —

"We often feel as if we're on a hamster wheel, running hard and getting nowhere fast! Legions of angels surround us at all times, eager to help — if only asked. Nothing is too small or too great. They provide Divine Guidance by dropping clues throughout each day. They are anxious to help, even with discovering our Divine Purpose. All we need do is stop and open ourselves to hear their messages of love and acceptance."

Teresa Christian has been a Life Purpose Coach for ten years and is both a certified Angel Card Reader and Passion Test Facilitator. TheAngelElement.com

My Inspired Thoughts

— DAY 97 —

My Inspired Thoughts

— DAY 98 —

"You become truly empowered when you believe in your dreams, both consciously and subconsciously. Always remember that your thoughts and feeling materialize, and they move more mountains than actions alone. Let all that you do, think, or say be infused with love, and let God light up a path of abundance for you.

Let your inner child bring forth your ancient wisdom. Live in an inspired state of mind, and you too will feel timeless."

Alina Vasilenko - aka Alexis - is the author of the book series, "Mighty and Brennon," a comedy about cats. Alina writes comedy, children's and YA books.
WrittenStoryPlanet.com

My Inspired Thoughts

My Inspired Thoughts

— DAY 99 —

"Did you do everything right according to the rules of the LoA and got no or disappointing results? This is caused by DNA imprints owned or inherited, damage to your soul and negative emotions lingering on in your energyfield caused by emotional trauma. This forms your baseline for what you manifest.

Living your life from passion, joy and grattitude. Working on your goals with focus, letting them benefit yourself, others and the Earth catalyse it."

After near death, **Natasja Billet** started researching and began shifting her health and life. Now she's helping others shifting their lives so they can flourish.
LoATheSecrets@gmail.com

My Inspired Thoughts

— DAY 99 —

My Inspired Thoughts

"If you want to design your destiny and blaze a trail, you need to step into leadership.

Great leaders stand out from everyone else, including other leaders; they copy no one. They differentiate themselves by being courageous and vulnerable. When they do, they generate unlimited opportunities and energize the people they are called to serve.

Is this you? Remember, comfort doesn't change the world. Vulnerability, however, changes everything."

Lisa Marie Platske, award-winning leadership expert and executive coach, speaks to mission driven entrepreneurs and executives on the importance – and power – of vulnerability in leadership. UpsideThinking.com

My Inspired Thoughts

— _DAY 100_ —

My Inspired Thoughts

— DAY 101 —

"Full potential. Truly believe that children/ youth are capable learners and recognize the potential in them, nurture that potential and watch the children/youth blossom.

Take these present moments and develop the potential within, that's how futures are created.

Sharing and transferring knowledge, keeps that knowledge alive and futures bright. In this process you may discover that there are some hidden potential in you too. Bring it out, develop it and let it shine!"

Patrice Porter is a Certified Educational Associate, Author of the Book Series "Bringing Out The Potential Of Our Children", Speaker, and Co-founder of WritersSecrets.com. FullPotential.co.place

My Inspired Thoughts

— *DAY 101* —

My Inspired Thoughts

— DAY 102 —

"We have been sold the idea of Success is the outward trappings: the cars, jewellery and houses. True Success doesn't mean having the most toys; it means having the self-confidence to be yourself and pursue your own dreams, no matter what others think. It's about being a successful human being, not just a successful human doing. It's just as much about relationships, personal and spiritual growth as it is about career and money."

Barbara Burgess ~ Hypnotherapist, Regression Therapist, NLP Master Practitioner, Speaker, Trainer, Author, and Success Coach using a unique, evidence-based blend of coaching, therapy, science and soul. BarbaraBurgess.com

My Inspired Thoughts

_____
_____
_____
_____
_____
_____
_____
_____
_____
_____
_____
_____
_____
_____
_____
_____
_____
_____
_____

— _DAY 102_ —

My Inspired Thoughts

— DAY 103 —

*"'Efficiency is doing things right; effectiveness is doing the right things,' Peter Drucker. Marketing effectiveness goes a step further and does the right things **at the right time.***

Most businesses start off solving a simple problem and aren't clear on the next steps. There is a phase of overwhelm and frustration as they try to grow. But when you create a business with a real strategy that meets your goals, you create profit and freedom."

Nancy Seeger, Speaker, Educator and Founder of Seeger Consulting Inc., a digital agency that optimizes marketing for maximum return and simplifies technology for business owners. SeegerConsultingInc.com

My Inspired Thoughts

— _DAY 103_ —

My Inspired Thoughts

"Human beings want to belong and desire connection. We want people to understand who we are. Hearing so many different voices, we lose ourselves in the crowd, and in the process, we drown out relying on our instincts. We have become people pleasers.

The beauty of life is traveling the road to self-discovery and defining yourself. Be less than what others tell you that you should be. Discover and become more of who you are."

Marcia McCray is the Founder of The Brand Naked Agency™ and Author of *The Busy Entrepreneur's Guide To Developing A Brand In 60 Days Or Less.*
TheBrandNakedAgency.co

My Inspired Thoughts

— DAY 104 —

My Inspired Thoughts

"Commitment — doing what you said you would do in all aspects of your life. However, we all know it doesn't work this way all the time. To live a committed life you must be true to yourself, you must be sincere.

*If you're sincere about what needs to be done or what you want in life you will find a **way**, if not you will find an **excuse**. Choose to find the way."*

David Scarborough is the Founder/President of Strategic Marketing Advisors, LLC, a well-respected Phoenix-based consultancy and Co-author of *The Procrastinator's Guide To Marketing*. StrategicMarketingAdvisors.com

My Inspired Thoughts

— _DAY 105_ —

My Inspired Thoughts

"It sounds obvious, but to be able to help people, you have to genuinely want to help people!

If everything you put out into the world is for your own gain, you will reach no one, and you will not change any lives.

Authentically share your knowledge and passion, create value for people without being asked, and over deliver. You can only help people who believe in you as a person and trust your expertise!"

Nikki Dalby is a Nutrition Coach, Personal Trainer and Blogger who has a passion for helping people feel their best and for creating sustainable healthy lifestyles.
kineticstrengthconditioning.com

My Inspired Thoughts

— _DAY 106_ —

My Inspired Thoughts

"Never be afraid to erect walls you will break. No one gets it on the first try, no matter. Never be afraid to rank number two. Try and fail. Fail better. Grow. Find your path. Those who succeed are those who never give up, never stop trying, do not mind falling, do not mind going back to the starting line. It's there for you to learn. See? Do not disappoint."

Sussu Leclerc is a Fiction Writer, Teacher and Writer at "The Winged Pen." Sussu has been helping the writing community for years, at <u>NovelWithoutFurtherAdo.weebly.com/</u>

My Inspired Thoughts

— *DAY 107* —

My Inspired Thoughts

"What you do matters! I experienced a difficult time: divorce, job ending and other life items at once. Although I felt adrift without an anchor people stepped forward in miraculous ways. My friends called and checked on me; my colleagues insisted I come for free healing sessions. No matter how dark the days, people offered me love and I felt treasured. When someone is having a rough time – connect - it can change their life."

DEBBI DACHINGER: Media Personality interviewed on over 800 media outlets. A syndicated, award-winning radio host, red carpet interviews, keynote speaker, certified coach, international bestselling author. DebbiDachinger.com

My Inspired Thoughts

— DAY 108 —

My Inspired Thoughts

— DAY 109 —

"Seeds Not Leads ~ When starting on your purpose work journey it is critical to learn quickly how to get out of your own way, surrender and do business the 'spiritual way'.

Your job is to plant spiritual seeds, not gather business leads. Where you plant may not be where you harvest but know that one tiny seed can produce an abundance.

Have Faith; everything you need and desire to fulfil your purpose will be provided."

Lisa Ormenyessy: Business Consultant and Intuitive Artist capturing your spirit's beauty on canvas. Remember, Re-energize and Reconnect to your most precious self with just one look. VibaliciousArt.com/spiritualjourney

My Inspired Thoughts

— _DAY 109_ —

My Inspired Thoughts

— DAY 110 —

"What if the symptom you have spent months resisting is actually your doorway to access your innate wisdom to guide you back to health?

Time to trust your body! It is your best friend trying to get a powerful message to you! Listen to it, engage with its healing energy through unfolding sensations, feelings and images which will allow the natural resolution of the energetic layers that are interfering with the natural flow of health."

Martine M.L. Negro: Co-founder of the Energetic Healing Diploma; Vice President of the Dowsers Society of NSW; Author of *Hacking the Wellbeing Code through Energetic Intelligence*. MartineNegro.com

My Inspired Thoughts

— *DAY 110* —

My Inspired Thoughts

— DAY 111 —

"When you're in resistance - be still and ask - What's right about this that I'm not getting..? Everything in your life is designed to bring you to your greatness. Your inner path of knowing your Infinite Being State. Have faith when you cannot see clearly the reasons for happenings you deem as disharmonious; for there is always a greater purpose for fulfilment of the divine order at work."

Anita Wisdom: Transformational Coach, Quantum Healer, and Author. She specializes in helping others discover and live their Soul Purpose with ease. AnitaWisdom.com

My Inspired Thoughts

— *DAY 111* —

My Inspired Thoughts

"We have the ability to live a vibrant, joyous life in health and wellness.

Wellness is not a static state. It's a continuous life long process of self-examination, awareness and action. Having knowledge or awareness is not enough for change to occur. Change needs action. We are all capable of making incredible changes to improve our lives. Move forward one step at a time. As long as you are moving, you are making progress."

Jinji Dissanayake: Wellness Advocate & Educator, Author, International Speaker, Founder of Simply Well Fed, which promotes healing nourishment for the body, mind and spirit. SimplyWellFed.com.au

My Inspired Thoughts

— *DAY 112* —

My Inspired Thoughts

"You didn't come into this world to be ordinary. You came to bring change, if even in the smallest ways. The more you know who you are and what you stand for, the greater your ability to stand true. Authenticity becomes a powerful tool for creating miracles, but you can't fake it. Your presence becomes the catalyst for others to get in touch with and show up as their true selves, eliminating the pretense that disconnects us."

Lorrie Kazan was chosen as one of the top psychics in a worldwide audition for Edgar Cayce's *Association for Research & Enlightenment.*   ILoveMyPsychic.com

My Inspired Thoughts

— *DAY 113* —

My Inspired Thoughts

— DAY 114 —

"Warm air. Hard concrete under my feet, now it changes to soft grass, then to gravel, making a crunching sound in the morning quiet. Quivering becomes apparent through the harness. Her head turns toward the robin singing, watches the squirrel scamper, soft whines. All this I experience through senses other than sight, and also through the eyes of Maggie, my Doberman Pinscher guide dog. Through her eyes, I see the world – Miracles happen daily!!!"

Caitlyn Furness is a pet coach who lives in Ontario with her husband, three cats, and two guide dogs. Caitlyn enjoys reading, nature, and music. CaitlynFurness.com

My Inspired Thoughts

— DAY 114 —

My Inspired Thoughts

— DAY 115 —

"Hope is for pessimists. Faith is for optimists. Are you hoping 'I am the missing piece the world needs' or do you know 'I am the missing piece the world needs?' Have faith that your life mission is stronger than your fear. You'll rarely fulfill your mission, relying on hope alone. Hope is fragile because hope walks hand-in-hand with fear in forecasting the future and ruminating the past. Faith is all-in.... Are you in?"

Sharon Sayler MBA, **PCC**, Trainer, Speaker, Best-Selling Author, has been affectionately dubbed the "Difficult People Whisperer" because she shows you how to be a courageous communicator. Download her eBook: SharonSayler.com/Gift

My Inspired Thoughts

— DAY 115 —

My Inspired Thoughts

— *DAY 116* —

"Don't Fear Contrary Opinions ~ The Founding Fathers disagreed vehemently with one another about the definition of 'America.' They did not shrink from these debates nor stifle contrary opinion. They welcomed diverse opinions and created a country comprised of the best of all opinions. Free speech means freedom to hold and express contrary opinions. We cannot ridicule or shout down or suppress diverse opinions. To be 'American' is to encourage, embrace and understand all opinions."

Mike Nemeth is a Writer and the Author of the best-selling legal thriller *Defiled* and its soon-to-be-released sequel, *The Undiscovered Country.*   nemosnovels@gmail.com

My Inspired Thoughts

— *DAY 116* —

My Inspired Thoughts

"Your thoughts and emotions impact your physical body and overall health.

There are times in your life when you deal with problems that cause you emotional upset in some way. Being upset is a reaction indicating there's conflict inside. Conflict can be expressed within your body in the form of aches/pains, your mind in the form of negative thoughts/emotions and your spirit as unrest. Resolve the conflict inside and you heal your body, mind and spirit."

Sheila Unique is a Medical Intuitive, Transformation Coach, Trainer, Speaker, CEO/Founder of The Unique Approach and an Expert in the field of teacher and student achievement. TheUniqueApproach.com

My Inspired Thoughts

— DAY 117 —

My Inspired Thoughts

— DAY 118 —

"If I asked you to write 3 things you like about yourself, would you be able to? Having confidence and a positive self-esteem would help, right?

When those around you are constantly bullying you, it would be hard to think positively about yourself.

Serving others, developing your own mantra - I am worthy - and finding a fun hobby are 3 ways to gain confidence and a better self-esteem. ***I*** *decide my own value and worth!"*

Tammy Atchley is an aspiring Author, Coach and Workshop Host. Married the love of her life 22 years ago and they have 4 children. TammyAtchley.com

My Inspired Thoughts

— *DAY 118* —

My Inspired Thoughts

"You are a leader when you influence people. You will have followers, and they, in turn, will have them too. You will not only influence them but also, as a consequence, will create an impact on your environment and that of your followers and the followers of your followers. The world will never be the same. You will have created a legacy. For that to happen, start by becoming the leader of your own self!"

Sally Bendersky, Founder of New Leadership, Best-Selling Author, Chemical Engineer, Ambassador, Industry leader, and certified Coach, has helped transform hundreds of lives and leadership performance. TheNovelEntrepreneur.com

My Inspired Thoughts

— _DAY 119_ —

My Inspired Thoughts

— DAY 120 —

"You can invest all you want into your business, retirement plan, real estate, etc., but failure to invest in your own education will always hold you back. It is amazing to meet entrepreneurs with lofty goals and dreams who refuse to invest in their own education to achieve these lofty goals and dreams. Understand this. There is no greater investment out there than your own education- take it from somebody who invests for a living."

Zubin Farhad Sethna is a Passive Income Professional, International Best-Selling Author, Award-Winning Speaker, and Business Coach. ZubinSethna.com

My Inspired Thoughts

— _DAY 120_ —

My Inspired Thoughts

— DAY 121 —

"You are enough! You are the secret to the good life! When you are your true self and live in alignment with that, you will create the life you desire. Invoke your true essence – DIVA, QUEEN and GODDESS.

The #1 thing that pulls you away from being your true essence is STRESS! Stress drains your energy, blocks your power and signals a shift is needed. Do you know how stress is stopping you?"

La Shonda Herring is the Transformational Goddess, Author, Speaker, Founder of The H Zone. The Sacred Tribe helps women invoke their true essence to create the life they desire. TheHZone.com

My Inspired Thoughts

— _DAY 121_ —

My Inspired Thoughts

— DAY 122 —

"Do not own what is not yours to own.

Some things we need to own like accepting praise or admitting our mistake. Assuming someone close to you is angry, sad or unhappy because of your actions or behaviour, without evidence; is owning their negative thoughts and feelings. What would your life look like today if you only owned what was yours to own?"

David Lawson is a Clinical Counsellor/Life Coach who works with people to help them to stop owning what isn't theirs to own. FindingtheLight.com.au

My Inspired Thoughts

— *DAY 122* —

My Inspired Thoughts

— DAY 123 —

 *"Your past doesn't have a future, but you do! Looking back in life is acceptable so you can see everything you have accomplished and recognized how far in life you have not only survived but also thrived. Move forward in life with positive intentions so you can be an encourager and set examples for others to follow. Do something today, tomorrow, and next week that will assist you to Persevere Past your Paralysis."*

Dr. James M. Perdue, a Quadriplegic from a football game, is a Speaker, Author, Successful Educator and Championship Coach. He speaks on ABC's Accept Adversities, Begin Battle, and Conquer Challenges.   JamesPerdueSpeaks.com

My Inspired Thoughts

— _DAY 123_ —

My Inspired Thoughts

— DAY 124 —

"Are You M.I.A.? Are you present in your life or missing in action?

Life is for living fully in the here and now with love, peace and joy.

Fully engage in life by living each moment fully present and acknowledge God's beauty and abundance existing in this world.

Stand up and be yourself and be proud of who you are, as you are a shining light in this world. Be Present. Be Love. Be You."

Shona Battersby is a Spiritual Healing and Transformational Guide using Reiki, Massage and Crystals and other tools. ShonaBattersby@littlebearmedicine.co.business

My Inspired Thoughts

— _DAY 124_ —

My Inspired Thoughts

— DAY 125 —

"Divine Dark. Spiritual oxymoron, or forgotten truth?

Western mythologies and media have expertly cultivated a dense thicket of conditioned fears that malign Dark as Evil and block our innate desire for the soothing, restorative powers of the Dark.

Unrelenting Light, though, is blinding and overpowering, searing rather than healing. A conscious practice of relaxing into the healing embrace of the Divine Dark can relieve the overwhelm of over-Lighting, to softly restore your balance—and your soul."

Susan V. Sinclair, Soul Reader and Sound Healer, Spiritual Intuitive, Speaker and Workshop Leader, Unabashed Mystic and Unboxed Oracle, Founder of GraceFlow Healing Arts. SusanSinclair.org

My Inspired Thoughts

— _DAY 125_ —

My Inspired Thoughts

"Everything contains the essence of light. So every situation, thought, emotion, problem... literally everything contains its core light within.

And where is light, there is no limit. There is freedom; simply, because you can see everything thoroughly. When you realize this simple truth, there is no fear anymore. Therefore you can make a change: 'I'm beyond limitation. I allow myself to transform into the fullness of health, love and prosperity right here and now.'"

Barbara Lukowiak is an interpreter of the language of light for all, who wish to unlock their inner strength and share it with other beings. BarbaraLukowiak.com

My Inspired Thoughts

— _DAY 126_ —

My Inspired Thoughts

— DAY 127 —

"Above all else, be open-minded to what life has to offer. You don't know where inspiration or help will come from.

Be honest with yourself. Opportunities in life are easier to recognize when you accept and are true to yourself.

Be caring and supportive of others and they will be caring and supportive of you.

Know that there is always guidance out there, wherever life takes you, if you are willing to accept it."

Sharon Richmond, MBA, RD, LDN, CLT, is a Registered and Licensed Dietitian specializing in symptoms with chronic inflammation/pain, weight loss and bariatric surgery. NutritionYourWeigh.net

My Inspired Thoughts

— *DAY 127* —

My Inspired Thoughts

— DAY 128 —

"Don't ever give up on your dreams! No matter your age, you can always learn and do anything you choose to. Age isn't a detriment but a knowledgebase of experiences to draw from. I'm a 64-year-old late-blooming author and will soon have my first novel released. Winston Churchill said: 'Never give up on something you can't go a day without thinking about.'

Keep (your dream) trucking! Haul your dream all the way to its fulfillment destination!"

Kelly Mack McCoy is the Author of the soon-to-be-released book *On The Road Again*, Semi-Retired (Pun Intended) Over-The-Road Trucker. Follow Mack's adventures at OntheRoadAgainNovel.com.

My Inspired Thoughts

— _DAY 128_ —

My Inspired Thoughts

"Welcome to the Transformational Times... when navigating life feels a bit like whiplash. But this also means that more individuals are seeking answers and are willing to hear from people who have established track records as authorities, experts, coaches and mentors. They are more open to new ways of doing things, new ways to view and live in the world. So step up Transformation Agent! Our world needs you! This is your call to action!"

Jackie Lapin, founder of <u>SpeakerTunity.com</u>, providing direct contacts for authors and leaders to book themselves on stages, radio shows, podcasts and virtual summits.

My Inspired Thoughts

— *DAY 129* —

My Inspired Thoughts

"Everything starts within.

Rather than going into something expecting yourself to be, allow yourself to become. It is a practice of self-acceptance, awareness, and curiosity which will shift your energy forward into a place of positivity and openness. What if things were done for you, rather than to you? What could be learned in each experience? How you do anything is how you do everything, first to yourself and then to others."

Susanne Cordes-Hoelterhoff, CPCC, ACC, cross-cultural executive and leadership coach & trainer, deep listener, tough questions asker, passionate bridge builder, and co-daredevil at TeamEssenz-Coaching.com.

My Inspired Thoughts

— DAY 130 —

My Inspired Thoughts

— DAY 131 —

"Think about the progress you've made, not the goals you've missed. No matter what you are trying to accomplish, new habits that you may never have previously considered must be adopted. Learning new ways to do things... to achieve your goals and desires will fill you with positive energy to enjoy your life. Yes, you may fail; but never give up! Life is an ever-evolving journey.

It's all about progress, not perfection!"

Cassandra Schmigotzki, NETA-CGEI Certified Wellness Coach/Founder of The Long and Winding Road to Wellness, helps struggling women eliminate emotional eating to regain control and enjoy life.　lawrtw.com

My Inspired Thoughts

— *DAY 131* —

My Inspired Thoughts

— DAY 132 —

"Are YOU The Missing Piece to the Puzzle?

What I love about this concept is that we are all unique. It is precisely your uniqueness that makes the world (puzzle) a better place. When you can embrace your uniqueness, rather than criticize it, you will truly get the importance of your inclusion into this world masterpiece. So love who you are and send out that love so that all our uniqueness becomes one."

Lynda Dyer is a 9 time International Best-Selling Author, Coach and Master NLP Trainer. Linda is passionate about assisting people to realize their own magnificence and share it. MindPowerGlobal.com.au

My Inspired Thoughts

— <u>DAY 132</u> —

My Inspired Thoughts

"The concept of productivity has evolved over the years. It's not about doing more in less time anymore.

The most successful people in the world are now the ones who can easily determine if a task is really worth their time. Just like them, we have to become masters at prioritizing which actions are necessary to achieve our goals.

Let's redefine the term productivity. It is not about time management anymore, it is about priority management.

Catherine Lefebvre-Babinsky, Reformed Procrastinator, Professional Problem Solver, Productivity Expert, Book Fanatic and Founder of The Clever Achiever: helping business owners to optimize their productivity. TheCleverAchiever.com

My Inspired Thoughts

— DAY 133 —

My Inspired Thoughts

— DAY 134 —

"Ancient scriptures remind us that by the grace of God we each have a highly unique gift destined to be brought joyfully into the world. Do you know your divine purpose and your unique gift? Surprisingly, it is all encoded in your date of birth and your given birth name!

I'd love to guide you to REMEMBER, REVEAL and EMBODY your highest, passionate gift/purpose in this lifetime. You and your gift are the missing piece!"

Hal Price is a Master Numerologist, Interfaith Minister, Owner of the HALgorithm™ Divine Destiny Program, Int'l Award-Winning and Best-Selling Author/Inspirational Speaker and a volunteer for the Teddy Bear Cancer Foundation. HalPrice.org

My Inspired Thoughts

— *DAY 134* —

My Inspired Thoughts

"Each of our acts makes a statement as to our purpose." ~ Leo Buscaglia

"The movie, It's a Wonderful Life, *illustrates very powerfully how our lives are intrinsically interwoven. The story reminds us that we are often blind to our value to others and our own self-worth. We may not be able to see from our limited perspective the profound impact we have on those around us. Believe in yourself – YOU matter!"*

Linda Valente M.Ed, MFT specializes in coaching women recovering from abusive relationships rediscover their power and their voice. <u>LindaValenteCoaching.com</u>

My Inspired Thoughts

— DAY 135 —

My Inspired Thoughts

— *DAY 136* —

"You spend roughly 1/3 of your life at work. You will be much happier at work if your job aligns with your interests, skills, and values.

Finding work you actually like is a process. First, understand what makes you tick, your unique talents, and what is important to you. It's then easier to decide on the next steps in your career.

You are unique and valuable: you have a distinctive mix of skills to offer!"

Lydia Newell is a career success coach, helping millennials figure out what they want to be now they're grown up. LydiaCareerPlanner.com   (Photocred: Hannah Soar)

My Inspired Thoughts

— *DAY 136* —

My Inspired Thoughts

— DAY 137 —

"Our magnificent lives are made of precious moments. In our moments, we make our choices.

For instance, if we choose to be authentic service-based professionals - then acute awareness for adding real value with heart, meaning, and productive actions, can vibrate with others through a unifying deep emotional and soul connection. Leading to awakening daily with a cause and plan to be the best we can be in all areas of our lives."

Terry Marsh, a Coach, Trainer, Speaker, Award-Winning Sales Person, and Conference MC, helps others flip the switch to awakening and achieving their dreams.
SalesPartnersCapetown.co.za

My Inspired Thoughts

— *DAY 137* —

My Inspired Thoughts

— _DAY 138_ —

"Capitalize on Creativity ~ Plan a creative activity into your weekly routine, whether it is coming up with a new form to expedite your work or preparing for an upcoming event or updating your website with new graphics...or planting flowers in your yard. This can be like a fresh breeze in the midst of necessary but maybe less enjoyable tasks associated with your business."

Holly Bundrant, PhD, RD, LDN is a registered dietitian and the founder/owner of Hope & Health Nutrition Services.   CookevilleNutrition.com

My Inspired Thoughts

— _DAY 138_ —

My Inspired Thoughts

— DAY 139 —

"Words are the most powerful force known to humankind. A kind word, a cross word, invokes perplexing emotions, unfathomable without a heart. Stop, pause, look around, and marvel at the space around you. This is your space, your moment. Make it count by ensuring your every word paints a picture of you. Be forever whom you are, false perceptions need not trouble your soul. Remember, there's only one of you. Let the True You Shine."

Francis Heran, Internationally Recognized Author and Mental Health Advocate, Saves lives by providing guidance and support and goes wherever needed because every person matters. HeranCreations.com

My Inspired Thoughts

My Inspired Thoughts

"Was your curiosity peaked by this book's title? I daresay, make it a declaration - you ARE a missing piece!

After a near-death experience, I know this is true. You were born with a gift, unique to your purpose and contribution. People need what you bring to our evolving humanity.

Believe in your greatness, never give up in discovering your gift, and leave your lasting legacy! This will fulfill you and the world will be better because you've lived."

Dr. Tianna Conte, Transformational best-selling Author and trailblazing blend of mystic and scientist. With 40 years of expertise, she empowers self evolution by re-awakening innate guidance and power.   YourGPSCode.com

My Inspired Thoughts

— _DAY 140_ —

My Inspired Thoughts

"Success is your birthright! Get clear on the vision for your life then act. As you walk toward your goals, you will define and refine the steps required to make your vision a reality. It is an evolving process. Believe in your vision and keep moving forward. If one step in your vision turns into a roadblock, move forward to the next. When you keep moving toward your goals, you will always win!"

Charmagne Coston is a Best-Selling Author, Speaker, and Owner of Branch Out Solutions. A company dedicated to helping small businesses and entrepreneurs succeed. BranchOutSolutions.com

My Inspired Thoughts

— *DAY 141* —

My Inspired Thoughts

"Stress is not always bad. The flight/ freeze/fight response is not some outdated condition that we have evolved past. It very much affects our modern lives and is NECESSARY. However, we need to find and reduce the sensitivity of our triggers when conditions are not life threatening. Chronic stress affects us physically, mentally and emotionally. The additional strain increases the pain on all levels. Reduce the stress, reduce the pain."

Lynn Jasmin is an Author, Trainer, Speaker, and Stress Reduction Specialist. <u>RelaxedFreedom.com</u>

My Inspired Thoughts

— _DAY 142_ —

My Inspired Thoughts

"'When the road less traveled doesn't work, create your own path.'

When the metaphorical 'road less traveled' won't benefit you and your dreams, you may have to create your own road from scratch. I Googled 'singing travelogue' and found nothing. It was the most terrifying and exhilarating moment in my life. But that dream gave birth to a successful business, and I'm now able to share a part of America's history that isn't found in a book."

Cecelia "Cece" Otto, professional singer, author, historian, and speaker, Founder of An American Songline®, which shares America's history through song and story.
AmericanSongline.com

My Inspired Thoughts

My Inspired Thoughts

— DAY 144 —

"We are living in such a challenging, revolutionary and yet precious time.
A time like never before.
It's our job to remember there's more to see than meet the eyes. It's our responsibility to look for and remember who we really are, reconnect to our higher self, find within the Peace and Love of God.
We're in charge of shifting our reality, now. Take the first step of your inner sacred journey today."

Elisa Palma Hancock, Spiritual Life Coach and Teacher, Akashic Records Consultant, and Author.
ElisaPalmaHancock.com

My Inspired Thoughts

— DAY 144 —

My Inspired Thoughts

" 'Humor is mankind's greatest blessing.'
~ Mark Twain

Laughter is more powerful than most people realize. It is nature's medicine for the soul. If you develop an appreciation and understanding of the value of humor then you will gain a healthier perspective on life. Enhance your life with humor! Be willing to laugh at yourself when those chances arise. Cultivate humor in your life and of those around you and discover its magic. "

Robert Slotta is an Author, Speaker, Nationally Recognized Mark Twain Historian & Memorabilia Specialist, Founder of Admirable Books, Discoverer of Twain's secret sequel to *Huckleberry Finn*. HowHuckFooledHemingway.com

My Inspired Thoughts

— DAY 145 —

My Inspired Thoughts

"You. Your own uniqueness. Your life and life experiences happen for a reason. Your successes and failures are lessons you can share to help and empower others who enter into your realm of influence.

Keeping your stories to yourself serves no one. Please Do Not take Your wisdom to the grave with You. When will you share your story? What are you waiting for?"

Tamia Dow is an award-winning international best-selling author, speaker, trainer and coach. She helps authors write their life stories and share them through books. TamiaDow.com

My Inspired Thoughts

_____
_____
_____
_____
_____
_____
_____
_____
_____
_____
_____
_____
_____
_____
_____
_____
_____
_____

— *DAY 146* —

My Inspired Thoughts

— DAY 147 —

"My purpose is to entertain, educate and inspire people to reach their potential. Someone is waiting for what we have to offer. Consider the questions asked of me by a customer at a convention display. 'Why haven't I heard of you? Why don't I know you? This information is exactly what I need.' Someone is waiting for exactly what we have to offer, how long will we make them wait?"

Orlando Ceaser, Best-Selling Author, Speaker, Publisher, Poet, Cartoonist, Voice-over Specialist, Creator of the Know System™ Decision Making Model and Ozone Leadership™. OrlandoCeaser.com

My Inspired Thoughts

— DAY 147 —

My Inspired Thoughts

— DAY 148 —

"How are you choosing to show up for the world? Our greatest asset is our attitude and the biggest gift we can give of ourselves is authenticity. Be you; be vulnerable enough to wear your heart on your sleeve, choose to live from a place of service, and contribution. It is not about what happens to us, it is about how we respond. We get to decide who we're going to be. Decide to be the missing piece."

Danielle Corenchuk MPAS, CPC, C.Ht. is an Int'l Best-Selling, Award-Winning Author, PTSD Specialty Coach, Trainer, Speaker, Philanthropist and Founder of Your Moment in Life Coaching & Personal Development.
YourMomentinLifeCoach@gmail.com

Inspired Thoughts

— *DAY 148* —

My Inspired Thoughts

"Gratitude and thankfulness are missing ingredients in many lives today. We prefer to grumble, complain, and criticize. When you begin your day thanking the Lord for His kindness, mercy, grace, and love, it impacts your attitude, thoughts, words, and actions.

I start and end every day the same way: 'Thank you, Lord, for giving me this day.'

It's a choice that I make every day.

What choice will you make today?"

Michael DeLon is an author, speaker, marketing coach, and the Founder/President of Paperback Expert, a marketing-centric book publisher.   PaperbackExpert.com

My Inspired Thoughts

— _DAY 149_ —

My Inspired Thoughts

— DAY 150 —

"When was the last time you took some time to just BE HERE NOW, and breathe?

What if, just for this moment, you stopped looking for answers, resources and solutions outside yourself, striving to have more, be more, and do more?

What if, when feeling tempted to panic, you took time to pause and become still, and listened to what you know to be the most empowering choice in that moment?"

Sarah Schweikert, is the Founder of Emerging Lotus, and helps people find empowerment and ease - by being fully present in the 'now' and acting in alignment with inner wisdom. Emerging-Lotus.com

My Inspired Thoughts

— _DAY 150_ —

My Inspired Thoughts

"Descartes said, 'I think therefore I am.' Most people believe it is themselves who is thinking. When, due to stress, they think negatively or get annoyed at every tiny upset and everyone; they believe they, themselves, must be faulty.

Meditation can reduce your stress overload and change your relationship with the mind so you can free yourself of the faulty thinking of believing you are your thoughts! On the way, you can attain peace."

QC Ellis is a Meditation and Personal Growth Coach and Author. Royalties from his first book, *Overcoming Anxiety* go to a charity helping people with anxiety and depression. QCEllis.com

My Inspired Thoughts

My Inspired Thoughts

— DAY 152 —

"Many go through life driven and tossed with the wind as they drift along the current, wondering where life will take them. There are some, who paddle through life knowing it's not the pull of the tides or the blowing of the winds that matters most; it's the set of their sail, their drive and ability to navigate life's storms, and where they choose to go as they create ripples in their wake!"

Jason Westover, Int'l Best-Selling Author, Speaker, and Founder of TurningPassionIntoProfit.com. Helping people who struggle increase their income and transform their life to one of purpose.

My Inspired Thoughts

— _DAY 152_ —

My Inspired Thoughts

"You're a divine creation
You're a gift to this world
You have a message to share
A message love so pure

Sing Your Song
Sing Your Song
And the world will sing along

Your voice is needed
Your voice is unique
There's no one else like you
So we need you to speak

Sing Your Song
Sing Your Song
And the world will sing along

So every voice is heard in the symphony of Life!"

Orgena Rose is a Producer, TV Host, Author, Vocalist, Song-writer, who has appeared on Broadway, Carnegie Hall, *OPRAH*, Tony Awards, *Today Show* , PBS and *Conan*. SacredRoseProductions.com

My Inspired Thoughts

— _DAY 153_ —

My Inspired Thoughts

"The biggest difference between bestselling authors and those who wish they were is around 200-300 pages.

It's often said, 'You need to believe in yourself!' I don't disagree, but there's more. Whether or not you believe in yourself, action is what makes the difference between dreaming and living your dream. When you act, you make progress, and seeing this progress makes you believe. Do something toward your dream today... then notice what happens to your belief!"

Lesley Marlo is a Writer, Editor, Book Coach, Marketing Maven, Founder of ExpertCopy, Writing, Editing & Publishing Firm. "Communication is Creation." ExpertCopy.com

My Inspired Thoughts

— _DAY 154_ —

My Inspired Thoughts

— DAY 155 —

~ Words to Live By ~

"'Say YES and work out the details later.' Face your fears and be exposed to interesting and fabulous opportunities. Learn gratitude.

'Look after your reputation!' - the world is so small; you will always run into your past.

'Never say anything about anyone you wouldn't be prepared to say to their face.' This speaks for itself.

Finally, from my mother, 'Why stand on the sidelines when you have the opportunity to dance?'"

Michelle Everingham, Lifestyle coach and mentor, small business owner. Bringing a world of experience to inspire and support women to achieve their desired personal and professional potential. MichelleEveringham.com

My Inspired Thoughts

— *DAY 155* —

My Inspired Thoughts

— DAY 156 —

"Life's a competition. With family, friends, strangers, and your peers. You should only be in competition with yourself. You are your best competition. Challenge yourself. Pick yourself up when life knocks you down. Become self-motivated, more knowledgeable. Reach your highest potential. Be selfish sometimes, because we are born into a selfish world. Just don't lose yourself in life trying to win over others. Celebrate personal victories, no matter how small. Mindfulness is key."

Shyla Burdine, Entrepreneur   madeselfmade@gmail.com

My Inspired Thoughts

My Inspired Thoughts

*"**Loving Thyself** ~ The need to feel loved is something we all share and while other people can bring us happiness, they can just as easily take it away. You are your best lover and cannot truly give others what you do not wholeheartedly give yourself. When inner happiness grows, it allows you to effectively share it with someone else."*

Desheen L. Evans, an Emergency/Trauma Recovery Coach and Senior-level Trainer. Creating visions for others to excel in life drives her success. EyesofPower.com

My Inspired Thoughts

— DAY 157 —

My Inspired Thoughts

— DAY 158 —

"One of the strongest ways to impact the world is to remain personally empowered. In order to remain empowered, staying present to the immediate moment and the truth of the reality of that moment is paramount. Ruminating in the past or projecting into the future is the fastest way to disempower oneself. In the present moment an appropriate response can become an infinite possibility to affect the future."

Kelly Lydick is a Meditation Facilitator, Reiki Master and Gateway Dreaming™ Coach, Author of *Mastering the Dream*, and member of the International Association for the Study of Dreams. KellyLydick.com

My Inspired Thoughts

— DAY 158 —

My Inspired Thoughts

— DAY 159 —

"Shine like a STAR ~ Your soul is the light that shines brightly in your heart and illuminates the world through your eyes.

What you choose to feel and express to the world matters!

What you choose to "see" and let others "see" about you matters!

Choose to "see" the light in others and in yourself!"

Susana Tuya Sarmiento, TV Presenter, Celebrity Speaker, Best Selling Author. Her true life mission is to create transformational change in people's lives and businesses. SusanaTuyaSarmiento.com

My Inspired Thoughts

— *DAY 159* —

My Inspired Thoughts

— DAY 160 —

"Believe, Act, Share: Don't be selfish — grab 60 seconds of insane courage and step up and share your message with those who need to hear it. When you have the confidence and self-belief to Believe in your message and your expertise, then add the strategies and techniques to Act on that belief to Share your message you become powerful.

Start today — take your first steps to be all that you can be — share your message."

Trish Springsteen is a multi-international award-winning speaker, mentor, author, radio host specializing in speaker training and Owner/Co-Founder of Trischel Innovative Communication Training. TrishSpringsteen.com

My Inspired Thoughts

— *DAY 160* —

My Inspired Thoughts

— DAY 161 —

"When you empower your soul to accept simple things such as love, joy, peace, thankfulness and kindness, your heart will connect your brain to experience a life of happiness and contentment. These spiritual values can be experienced without fear, greed or the yearnings for empty material-ism. Equally important, you are to have love for the creator, human race and for thyself. Above all, your thoughts, feelings and a peaceful mind can only bring you bliss."

Desziree Richardson is a Broadcastor/Media Personality, International Best-Selling Author and Board Member of Best-Selling Authors International Organization. Desziree.com

My Inspired Thoughts

— *DAY 161* —

My Inspired Thoughts

— DAY 162 —

"To live in happiness and joy, you must connect to the truth of your dreams in all areas of your life. Those dreams were given to you because you are the only one who can deliver those gifts. You are the one that carries the power to create all you desire. You are meant to have fantastic relationships and unlimited prosperity! Believe it and create it! You can have it all, now is your time!"

Mary Silver MSW, Published Author, Speaker, and Certified Life Coach helping women attract love, wealth, prosperity using positive psychology, LoA, Human Design, Astrology, and Numerology. MaryBaileySilver.com

My Inspired Thoughts

— _DAY 162_ —

My Inspired Thoughts

— DAY 163 —

"Dream Medicine ~ If dreams are to guide us, why don't they tell us simply what to do? Everybody dreams, but few remember them by morning. We know the creative potential of dreams, but few have experienced it directly. If dreams told us what to do, we would probably ignore their advice, as we often do elsewhere. Instead, the experience of the dream changes us. To learn from the medicine, honor the dream by some ritual action."

Henry Reed, Ph.D. is the "father of the modern dreamwork movement," by his creating the Sundance Community Dream Journal in 1976. <u>HenryReed.com</u>   (Photo by Janis Emeritus)

My Inspired Thoughts

— DAY 163 —

My Inspired Thoughts

"I have found and truly believe that this Universe meant for you to be happy, healthy and successful. Because... 'Within you, there is a place created for your dreams and goals.' This place is your innate Higher Potential, your Inner Light, it knows all and works through your subconscious mind. It is now up to you to activate your wish: Feel it in your heart. Focus. The Light listens and will help you to shine."

Rev. Dr. Helena Steiner-Hornsteyn, Int'l speaker, psychic healing coach, President of EnergyWorks International Inc. & Activale, and Best-selling author of *The White Light- A Limitless Reality.* <u>Activale.com</u>

My Inspired Thoughts

— _DAY 164_ —

My Inspired Thoughts

"Dance what you write. Move to increase creativity, vigor of prose, health, longevity, and to generate ideas. At least every hour you're writing, do interpretive dance. Dance the effect you want your readers to experience through your plot structure. Move the way a character in your fiction would move. Act the emotions or swelling tension of a scene. Walk around in the way your readers should walk after reading your non-fiction piece. Practice now!"

Tantra Bensko, Gold medal novelist of the Agents of the Nevermind psychological suspense series about social engineering, writing instructor with UCLA and elsewhere, manuscript editor. InsubordinateBooks.com

My Inspired Thoughts

My Inspired Thoughts

"Your Life is created like pieces of a jigsaw puzzle.

You may think that pieces are missing or not good enough.

In reality, they are parts of a magnificent puzzle you have to discover.

You are more than just a "Job name" or "Skill" or "Choice".

You are an incredibly complex, transformative mass of communication, procreation and co-creation.

Your life is a never-ending opportunity of discovering the unique pieces to your puzzle."

Jayc Ryder, Internationally Acclaimed Celebrity Psychic Medium, Author of 3 Intuitive Guidance Books, Online Entrepreneur, Speaker and Intuitive Coach Creating Clarity Through Conscious Connection. JaycRyder.com

My Inspired Thoughts

My Inspired Thoughts

— DAY 167 —

"Every moment we can choose to love ourselves better and shift our point of view to allow acceptance and inspired action. A singing rhyme can make it more fun.

'As we change the way we think

we change the way we feel.

If we make our mind our friend

we'll get a better deal.

Everyday we ride the waves of life's great mystery.

As we choose the path of Love we'll set ourselves free.'"

Laurie Roth (Lovefire), M.A. M.S, is a Licensed Marriage Family Therapist, Author, Sound Healer, Hypnotherapist, Joyshop Facilitator, Musician/Composer, Author, Performer and former radio-show host. <u>Lovefire.org</u>

My Inspired Thoughts

— _DAY 167_ —

My Inspired Thoughts

— *DAY 168* —

"Living a life on purpose and according to your vision means to commit wholeheartedly to your innermost values, your true essence and core passion. Your inner compass will guide you – and it will NOT always be comfortable. Living a full, panoramic life can be edgy at times – and this is good: go to the edge, as this is where the best view is. The ultimate adventure in life is to be authentically yourself – always."

Elisabeth Balcarczyk, M.A., PCC, Founder of Body Mind Soul Coaching, Transformational Leadership Workshops & Retreats Leader and Author based in Germany.
Coach_E_Balcarczyk@yahoo.com

My Inspired Thoughts

— *DAY 168* —

My Inspired Thoughts

— *DAY 169* —

"Often we are asked, "If you had a super-power, what would it be?" I believe the ability to speak up, whether for oneself, others or the environment, is one of our superpowers. Find the courage and you'll find the tools and teachers to help you develop the necessary skills to use your voice for good. Timely words well spoken are a superpower that can make a positive difference. Words have the power to improve lives."

Deanna Ford is an award-winning speaker, and the author of *Command the Stage: A Speaker's Guide to Using Notes Strategically to Develop and Deliver Better Speeches.*
DeannaFord.ca

My Inspired Thoughts

— <u>DAY 169</u> —

My Inspired Thoughts

— DAY 170 —

"Living in a globalized world is challenging, especially when we constantly collide with different cultures. Learn from that abundance of cultures and nationalities. See the unspoken. Allow cultural change to energize your life. Embrace it. Trust your intuition. Use your empathy. Be mindful and open to diversity-the outcome may surprise you. Always ask yourself how can I leverage cultural differences to increase my creativity, fulfilment and success?
Dare to be culturally aware. Thrive. Be exceptional."

Agata Szkiela, Intercultural Success Coach for spouses of diplomats and expats with 15 years of professional experience in diplomatic environment, UN and international corporations.   about.me/AgataSzkiela

My Inspired Thoughts

— _DAY 170_ —

My Inspired Thoughts

— DAY 171 —

"Your life, as an exquisite art masterpiece, is filled with imagination, creativity and inspiration. Stand in mindfulness always and bring your gifts to bear for the world and those around you. And like a great artiste, you will build your pallet of wondrous colors and paint with a numerous variety of brushstrokes filled with dreams and manifestations. Watch these manifestations ignite the passions in you and others. May you live your life artfully."

Dr. Janet Woods is a #1 Int'l best-selling author, award-winning speaker, media personality, and recipient of the US President's Lifetime Achievement Award for Community Service. JanetWoods.com

My Inspired Thoughts

— _DAY 171_ —

My Inspired Thoughts

— _DAY 172_ —

"The most powerful tool we have for enhancing youth and promoting health and vitality is our minds. If we think that disease and poor health is an intrinsic part of aging, it surely will be. If we say to ourselves, "I'm old," then our bodies will respond accordingly. Why not give permission to ourselves to be ageless? The first step is believing that we can. The fountain of youth is already inside of us!"

Eliza Morrison, A.K.A. "The Anti-Aging Analyst" is an anti-aging journalist and founder of The Ultimate Anti-Aging Arsenal Blog. AntiAgingAnalyst.com

My Inspired Thoughts

— *DAY 172* —

My Inspired Thoughts

"If you do not know where you are going, how are you going to get there?

You should always start with the end in mind. Dream, get clear on what you want your life to look like. Then base all decisions on your desires and you will always be moving towards your goals. Know the reasons why you want it, make it compelling. This will always keep you motivated and moving in the right direction."

Liza Sager, Certified Life Coach, strategic interventionist, survivor of domestic abuse and Founder of Success Sisterhood. YOU are the change you need.
WomansRockYourWorldCoaching.com

My Inspired Thoughts

— _DAY 173_ —

My Inspired Thoughts

"Is the missing piece within you your connection with your Divine Feminine Inner Wisdom? Seek her out. Go within and listen for her. Touch this energy of intuition, compassion, and love for all upon the earth. Sense this powerful inner guidance that will lead you to know your purpose, live from your true essence, and do your most fulfilling work. Set your intention to listen daily to your Divine Feminine Inner Wisdom. And keep listening."

The **Rev. Dr. Betty Powell** is a holistic psychotherapist, spiritual mentor, and creativity coach, empowering people to live by their own inner spiritual authority.
GroveTransformations.com

My Inspired Thoughts

My Inspired Thoughts

— DAY 175 —

"There is nothing better than being guided to do something by the wisdom that comes from your heart. You know that your heart is where your deepest truths lie and whenever you remain in that clear center not only do you feel more like yourself, there is also more harmony, more flow and even more success in your life. Take time to quiet your mind and listen to your heart!"

Heather Thomas is an Amazon #1 Best-Selling Author, a CranioSacral Therapist and Yoga Teacher. Heather offers different mentoring programs, classes and wellness events across Canada and around the world.   HeatherThomas.ca

My Inspired Thoughts

— *DAY 175* —

My Inspired Thoughts

— *DAY 176* —

*"The scales revealing our escalating weight and fat mass may terrify us! Faced with a **globesity epidemic,** what have we omitted in our efforts to reshape ourselves?*

*Hippocrates famously said, **'All disease starts in thy gut.'** Modern science adds, **Your brain has significant reasons for your adiposity.** YOU are the missing link in your own weight loss triumph. Metabolically unique — amidst master hormones controlling your fat-burning — it's time to stop battling the bulge. Instead, work with your body and brain!"*

Sarah Jane Michaels, "The Figure Queen" - 9 time #1 Int'l Best-Selling Author, Speaker, Weight Loss Expert. Pioneer of groundbreaking programs in digestive vitality, immediate and long-term weight loss success. WeightLossVitality.com

My Inspired Thoughts

My Inspired Thoughts

"We are taught to look to the external to value and understand who we are. Instead we must look to ourselves and have the courage to know what is important to us, no matter what anyone else says or does. This is true freedom, and allows our life of choice. By turning inward and make decisions from our heart and our feelings, we know the truth for ourselves. This is true choice."

Robyn McTague is a Master Holistic Healer who helps adults and children increase their vibration and create a life of choice and freedom. RobynMcTague.com

My Inspired Thoughts

— DAY 177 —

My Inspired Thoughts

— DAY 178 —

"We are given a special light with our first breath — a smile that comes as natural as a baby's and brings joy to others without conditions or doubts. As adults, the smile we share is a powerful loving light dissolving away worry, sadness, fears or anger. Be generous with your smiles because they will make someone's day happier as you embrace the joy of sharing your God-given talents."

Leticia Fuerte is a Best-Selling Author of her book, *Tarot and Angelic Tips (Tarot Y Consejos Angelicales)* and eCourses with meditations to cleanse/heal your personal energy. LeticiaFuerte.com

My Inspired Thoughts

— DAY 178 —

My Inspired Thoughts

"Happiness itself is a poor objective. When the journey is right, happiness appears automatically. Many short-term pleasures make us feel happy, but only while they last. And no matter how worthy, they seldom are what we would choose to be remembered by. Happiness comes to us when we use our capacities, in full integrity with our values, to pursue what we find truly worthwhile. Invariably those experiences and their results are what we're remembered for."

Robert Goldmann, Speaker, business and life coach, mindfulness teacher, and author of best-selling *Act from Choice: Simple tools for managing your emotions, your habits and yourself, to be how you mean to be.* ActFromChoice.com

My Inspired Thoughts

— _DAY 179_ —

My Inspired Thoughts

"It's never too late for love! You've felt disappointed and discouraged with dating and relationships. Don't give up on your dreams, settle for less, or resign yourself to living without love. You can achieve clarity about the right relationship for you, feel confident in yourself and your vision, and create a life you love, with the love of your life! Imagine how good you'll feel, living with joy, feeling cherished, and trusting you are loved!"

Dr. Wendy Lyon, Author, Speaker, Psychologist, and Master Certified Relationship Coach helping singles and couples create lives they love, with the love of their lives!
Dr.WendyLyon.com

My Inspired Thoughts

— DAY 180 —

My Inspired Thoughts

"It is not by the outward acquirement of facts that we become wise and great. The method of education to store the mind with as many facts as could be accumulated is conducive to knowledge learning. However, the method of education that leads to happiness is kindled from within oneself through an evolutionary inner journey. It is by developing the soul from within until it illuminates, that is the smartest investment in self. Be brilliant!"

DeNise N. Gore is a Certified Holistic Health Coach, Lifestyle Strategist, Author, Speaker & Founder of Radiant Brilliance – a personal development company.
RadiantBrillance.net

My Inspired Thoughts

— *DAY 181* —

My Inspired Thoughts

"Want to know who you really are? Ask yourself that while trekking, biking or hugging a tree. Reflect on the profoundness of life in stillness, meditation and nature.

For a moment, I was divinity tonight. Sacred tears are running down the face of this temple. To the depth of the abyss within, I am Peace. May Wisdom and Compassion start to fill the golden cauldron of my heart. For later, to overflow."

Steinar Almelid, military pilot and officer, poet and senior advisor to corporations and government organizations for strategy and leadership. SanataConsulting.com

My Inspired Thoughts

— _DAY 182_ —

My Inspired Thoughts

"Our bond was instant and life-changing. The love, trust and mutual healing Belle and I experienced saved both of us. Our relationship is one of the many examples of how it's not just about how animals make our lives better and how we can benefit from these relationships. Rather, it's about paying attention to what our animal friends are taking on when they help us, and healing each other through these genuine and unrivaled bonds."

Melissa Zine, LICSW, is a Certified Canine/Equine Massage Therapist, Energy Healer and Animal Communicator who integrates the power of healing through the animal-human bond. AnimalHumanHealingConnection.com

My Inspired Thoughts

— _DAY 183_ —

My Inspired Thoughts

— DAY 184 —

"Once upon a time I was Betty Badass! I was a Special Agent for the Bureau of Alcohol, Tobacco, Firearms & Explosives. Now retired, I struggled to find a purpose again and to figure out who I was without a badge. In Becoming Betty Badass, I found my purpose... to create and empower Badass women. Every woman has a Betty Badass in them, it's just a matter of unleashing her and that's where I come in!"

Amy Sue Michalik, Mastermind of Becoming Betty Badass, Retired Federal Agent, Author, Speaker, Screenwriter, Firearms Coordinator, NRA Firearms Instructor & *THE* Betty Badass. BecomingBettyBadass.com

My Inspired Thoughts

— _DAY 184_ —

My Inspired Thoughts

"Financial independence requires courage. Courage in Webster's Dictionary says 'the quality of being brave.' Being brave implies overcoming fear. But what do we fear – injury, damage, loss? Financial independence includes the courage to ask questions; and based on the information provided, choosing the best option to reduce your loss exposure. The only stupid question is the one not asked."

Donna Atkins is a Certified Public Accountant, Investment Advisor, Master Personal Financial Planner, artist, writer, photographer and producer. LightChannel@icloud.com

My Inspired Thoughts

— DAY 185 —

My Inspired Thoughts

"*A good leader should be a mentor, and I've always tried to be that. I had mentors who helped me through my early years, giving me the experience necessary to proceed. I try to share that with the team members with whom I work. Bounce innovative ideas off of them, see what their reaction is, and then listen to what they are saying. I always respected the team members' ideas and their competence — they were very bright individuals. I listened to what they had to say.*"

Terry Zweifel, Aerospace Engineer, #1 Int'l Best-Selling Author, responsible for 23 patents for safe air travel.
TerryZweifel.com

My Inspired Thoughts

— *DAY 186* —

My Inspired Thoughts

— DAY 187 —

"Throughout time, wise men, mystics and prophets advised us to love ourselves. Instead, we developed inner critics. Since we can only share what we have, we criticize others when mistakes occur. People don't need more critics; they're already their own biggest critic, which results in anger, disruption and rage.

The solution is developing unconditional love and acceptance for ourselves. Then acceptance and love is what we have to share. Harks back to 'Imagine' by John Lennon."

Joe Murphy, Entrepreneur, Student of Life and Founder of the "Game Changers," mentoring and empowering those receptive to developing unconditional love/acceptance for themselves. LivingFullTilt.com

My Inspired Thoughts

— _DAY 187_ —

My Inspired Thoughts

"What code do you live by? Does it consist of honesty, ethics, sincerity, honor, trust-worthiness, fairness, authenticity and integrity? Sounds impossible, doesn't it? Absolutely not! Choosing to adhere to this code enables you to be YOU at your great-est good. Each night when you go to sleep, you'll have peace of mind that you gave your very best. In today's world, this code is more important than ever. Living by this code will ripple out, affecting many."

Pam Murphy is an entrepreneur who empowers her clients to create their ideal businesses by removing the obstacles blocking their way.   pamurphy49@gmail.com

My Inspired Thoughts

— *DAY 188* —

My Inspired Thoughts

"Meet Bella. Bella started her journey in Georgia on a beautiful September morning. Her destination was North Carolina. This was accomplished through ten legs carefully planned by her rescue, 'New Rattitude'. Ten volunteers drove her, each for an hour or so, until she reached her foster family. When you think you aren't in a position to help whatever cause is close to your heart, remember this: 'No one can do everything, but everyone can do something.'"

Wendy Hancharick Rumrill has volunteered with animal rescue services for the past 7 years. Her most recent efforts are in the transport of rescue animals.
linkedin.com/in/wendyrumrill

My Inspired Thoughts

— *DAY 189* —

My Inspired Thoughts

About Expert Insights Publishing

Our mission is to give authors a voice and a platform on which to stand. We specialize in books covering innovative ways to meet the personal and business challenges of the 21st century.

Through our signature, inexpensive publishing and marketing services, we help authors publish and promote their works more effectively and connect to readers in a uniquely efficient system.

We employ an experienced team of online marketing strategists, ad copywriters, graphic artists, and Web designers whose combined talents ensure beautiful books, effective online marketing campaigns at easily affordable rates, and personal attention to you and your needs.

**We have promoted over 1,200 authors
to bestseller status.
Will you be next?**

Learn more about our current publishing
opportunities at:
ExpertInsightsPublishing.com

Made in the USA
Columbia, SC
05 November 2017